PRAISE FOR *THE FANTASY FALLACY*

"If we are going to positively impact our sexually broken society, we must become real and relevant. Reading *The Fantasy Fallacy* will help us do just that."

—Christine Caine
Founder, The A21 Campaign

"Pornography is poison. It peddles three toxic lies: Sex is cheap. Sex has no consequences. Sex requires no covenant. If our society continues to buy and believe these lies, then we can expect a slow, painful demise. It's not too late, however. But we must wake up and take a stand."

—Max Lucado
Pastor and best-selling author

"Thank God for Shannon Ethridge. In a world caught up with cravings for new and more exciting sexual experiences, Shannon writes a psychologically balanced and scripturally compatible book. You will find this response to what appears to be a universal mania to be enlightening and encouraging as well as affirming of healthy sexuality. I enthusiastically endorse this book."

—Marilyn Meberg
Author, *Constantly Craving*; and speaker, Women of Faith®

"It is not easy to swim against the current of popular culture. It isn't even necessary unless the current of popular culture is polluted, pulling good people to a place of pain and emptiness. *The Fantasy Fallacy* is more than a knee-jerk reaction to a harmless diversion. It is a well-researched rebuttal of a philosophy that is stealing *true intimacy* from the people who desire it most. Best of all, Shannon's book provides a clear map to a *real* place of sexual and personal fulfillment in the real world we live in: a place called *hope*."

—Ken Davis

Author, *Fully Alive*; and producer, SCORRE Conference

"Fantasy is tricky stuff—so tricky that it is seldom addressed. Shannon's approach is compassionate and compelling and, therefore, helpful. I'm impressed with her speedy and thorough response to this topic."

—Elisa Morgan

Author, speaker, and publisher, *FullFill*.org

"Sexual fantasies are normal—but for God-followers, often confusing. This book pulls back the curtains to reveal how we can use our sexual imaginations to enjoy true oneness with our spouses. Shannon Etheridge has shown light on a subject that too many have even feared to acknowledge. You don't want to miss her message."

—Drs. Les and Leslie Parrott

Authors, *Love Talk*

THE FANTASY FALLACY

Exposing the Deeper Meaning Behind Sexual Thoughts

Shannon Ethridge

THOMAS NELSON
Since 1798

NASHVILLE DALLAS MEXICO CITY RIO DE JANEIRO

Published in Nashville, Tennessee, by Thomas Nelson. Thomas Nelson is a registered trademark of Thomas Nelson, Inc.

Thomas Nelson, Inc. titles may be purchased in bulk for educational, business, fund-raising, or sales promotional use. For information, please e-mail SpecialMarkets@ThomasNelson.com.

To protect the privacy of clients, some names and details have been changed, and some stories are composite characters. All of the contextual elements and results, however, are true. Permission has been granted for use of real names, stories, and correspondence with some individuals.

Library of Congress Cataloging-in-Publication Data
Ethridge, Shannon.
The fantasy fallacy : exposing the deeper meaning behind sexual thoughts / Shannon Ethridge.
p. cm.
Includes bibliographical references.
ISBN 978-0-8499-6469-5 (trade paper)
1. Sex--Religious aspects--Christianity. 2. Sexual fantasies. I. Title.
BT708.E844 2012
241'.664—dc23

2012030004

Printed in the United States of America
12 13 14 15 16 OG 5 4 3 2 1

To my "Shrink Rap" friends,
Jarratt, Tom, and Cheryl

Contents

Acknowledgments

I never could have written a book about sexual fantasies were it not for the dozens of coaching clients willing to share the intimate details of their private thought lives. Thank you for your trust, courage, and humility.

And I couldn't have published such a book without a very courageous publisher behind me. Special thanks to Debbie Wickwire—my "angel with cowboy boots"—and the entire Thomas Nelson team for catching this vision and running with it. Joel Kneedler, thank you for believing in me and paving the way for this project.

When I started mentoring aspiring writers and speakers through the B.L.A.S.T. Program, I had no idea what a blessing it would become to *me*. Thanks to all of the B.L.A.S.T. participants who jumped into this manuscript headfirst with me! Lindsey Hartz, Carrie O'Toole, Christina Calk, and Sally Casanova—how I appreciate your countless hours of research assistance. Christy Kennard, Christy Johnson, Aniesha Kleinhammer, Aubrey Sampson, Crystal Sheren, and Rich Wildman—what a wonderful job you did providing editorial feedback every step of the way.

Several professional counselors and beloved colleagues were incredibly helpful in the development of this material, particularly Jarratt Major, Tom Haygood, Cheryl Mackey, Julianne Davis, and Chris Legg. Thank you for helping me help others while remaining true to God's Word.

There aren't words to express how grateful I am for the prayers of my family and more friends than could possibly be mentioned here. They have definitely sustained and strengthened me day by day.

To my closest friends who listened patiently (without cringing) as I've repeatedly shared my passion for this topic—Terrica Smith, Skyla Bradley, Jerry Speight, Rita Baloche, Nicki Bradshaw, Jim Bailey, and Marilyn Meberg—what phenomenal cheerleaders you've been, and I love you dearly for it!

Finally, I want to thank my husband, who has been so great at helping me expose the deeper meaning behind my own fantasies. Greg, I couldn't ask for a better life partner and friend.

Foreword

by Stephen Arterburn

Something is obviously very wrong today in relationships. I was having breakfast with a couple of guys recently—one was single, the other married. The single one was complaining about how hard it was to find a soul mate, a woman who would be interested in a guy like him.

He explained, "I'm not bad to look at, I have a good job and money in the bank, and I love God, but women don't seem to be satisfied with that. They fall for the bad guy—the one who treats them like trash. They say they want a nice guy, but they don't really. They think they can take a bad boy and turn him into a good guy. But considering some women's track records, that apparently *never* works. They keep getting their hearts ripped out and stomped on, and I keep wondering, 'What can't they see in a guy like *me*?'"

The married man chimed in, explaining that it was a little different at his house. His wife seemed to be in search of something more—something he didn't quite understand. She had been reading *Fifty Shades of Grey*, and he admitted that although her increased sexual interest was great, he was a little uncomfortable with certain expectations she had of how he should approach her and touch her, the exact words she wanted to hear, and the unusual sexual practices she was suggesting. It all seemed so "scripted," like a romance novel instead of real life. "She's always been satisfied before with our sex life, so I'm not sure what to make of it."

Perhaps men are getting a taste of what women have been complaining about for a long time. For years we have watched the integrity of men become consumed by the use of pornography. The Internet opened the doors to male eyes, and millions of men became hooked on depersonalized sexual experiences and self-gratification.

No woman can live up to the pornographic images on pages or in videos. The unreal drives out any hope for the real to be satisfying, so a man eventually gives up trying to replicate what he experiences with his porn. You could say that the pornographic fantasy world neuters the man and incapacitates his ability to have sex with a real, live human. Relationships are destroyed, and the man rationalizes away his shame. Anyone who has missed the proliferation of pornography use and addiction has missed one of the most destructive trends in the past twenty years.

It appeared that this type of isolative and divisive sexual practice would remain primarily a male problem. Though female pornography channels on television as well as online have experienced increased traffic, they have never been popular among women. They have not been accepted by the masses, nor are they gratifying to most women. So it looked as though women were safe from something as destructive as pornography. At least that seemed to be true until now.

When the Fifty Shades trilogy burst onto the scene, it became the topic of conversation in even the most conservative of circles. Erotic novels have been around for centuries, but never before have they been so accepted or read by so many. But the truth is these erotic books are dragging readers into a world of fantasy in a way very similar to how pornography hooks male viewers.

No man can create a sexual experience that parallels those in the books. No man can be viewed as adequate when compared to the erotic excitement found in these novels. The fantasy world that a woman enters will leave her very dissatisfied with the reality of her man and her marriage. The deeper into her fantasy world she goes, the more difficult it will be to experience sexual gratification in a real relationship, where the husband does not excite and stimulate with every move he makes or word he says. This kind of fantasy robs reality of any ability to satisfy.

A deeper explanation of the impact of sexual fantasy is needed—a more comprehensive examination of all dimensions of our sexual thought life. And that is why this book is so important. It could not come at a better time. Its subject matter has never been more relevant. It will help women *and* men—both married and single—to take a second look at the fantasy world they may be creating through romance novels, pornography, or their own imaginations. It will also help them get out of that fantasy world and back to building real, healthy relationships.

When the Every Man's Battle series became popular and helped so many men, there was an obvious need for something just as powerful to help women. I selected Shannon to author the Every Woman's Battle books, and she exceeded all expectations. There is no one better qualified to write about the topic of sexual integrity and sexual intimacy than Shannon. I think she will exceed your expectations, too, as she plows lots of new ground, exploring and revealing the truth about the destructive role that fantasy can play in a person's life.

I know that men don't typically read books written by women, but gentlemen, if I could urge you to make *one* exception, let it be *this* book. Shannon's wit, wisdom, and insight will *not* leave you disappointed.

So whether you are single or married, in a relationship or simply hoping to cultivate one in the future, read this book. It will prepare you for the rich, rewarding sex life that we all crave or help you repair the one you already have.

—Stephen Arterburn
July 2012

A Note to the Reader

Fifty Shades of Reality

My friend Natalie was the first to alert me to the existence of the Fifty Shades fiction trilogy by E L James. Through a brief e-mail she asked, "Have you seen this? It's about BDSM—bondage, domination, sadism, and masochism!" I didn't think much of it, until I started hearing more and more talk about it on television.

I saw an interview on our local news with a married couple. The wife was saying how she and her husband were reading the book together to create some steam in their sex life. He sat beside her nodding slightly, grinning from ear to ear, hand on her thigh. I thought, *Hey, that's great! I'm all about a married couple fueling their sexual energies for one another! Woohoo! Maybe we'll read it too!*

But as the media droned on about it, I noticed the interviews becoming slightly more hostile. Many folks were looking at the books through a completely different lens. "They're pornography . . . smut . . . trash!" many declared. I recognized those as fighting words and wondered what all of the hubbub was about.

When someone sent me a link to *Saturday Night Live*'s "digital short" spoof about *Fifty Shades of Grey*, my radar lit up. It aired around Mother's Day, featuring well-meaning husbands and children bringing gifts to Mom, only to discover her reading the book and masturbating in bed . . . in the bathtub . . . against the washing machine. *Hmmm*, I thought. *Obviously not* all *women are using the book to fuel their marriage bed. Some must be lighting their own fires and hiding the smoke signals from their husbands.*

I set a Google alert and began reading what others were saying about the series. Some insisted that reading the book was harmless. "Readers know the difference between truth and fiction!" was a common mantra from advocates. However, adversaries insisted, "If society believes this is what women want, we're in *danger*!" My red flag waved wildly when yet another Google alert revealed that sales of whips, chains, and other BDSM-related paraphernalia were on a drastic uphill climb . . . thanks to the Fifty Shades trilogy.

Soon the series had sold ten million copies within six weeks, and a friend told me there was a waiting list of more than four hundred people for the book at her local library. As I read blog post after blog post—some proclaiming the pros of the story, others crying out about the cons—I realized a culture war wasn't just brewing, it was already *raging*! And when I heard that a European hotel had replaced its Gideon's Bibles with *Fifty Shades of Grey* in all of its hotel rooms, I could only deduce that this isn't just a cultural war. It is a full-blown spiritual battle.

Although I didn't see the *Fifty Shades of Grey* onslaught coming, no doubt God did. And I think He let me feel the ground rumbling. For three years I'd been saying, "Someday I want to write about sexual fantasy!" And through all of the media madness and literary-critic chaos, I realized that the time for the book wasn't *someday*. It was *now*! Fortunately, I'd already read so many books, combed the professional research, conducted tons of interviews, and done lots of praying and soul-searching about where I stood on the matter of sexual fantasy.

Other than actually developing the manuscript, I knew I had one more bridge to cross. I had to actually read the Fifty Shades series. I couldn't write a response to something I had never read. My husband bought it for me, and we prayed that God would give me eyes to see it through *His* lens.

I confess I secretly hoped that it *would* throw gas on my already steady sexual fire for my husband, Greg. The verdict? It didn't affect me like I thought it would. I needed Greg to hold me, but not in response to sexual arousal on my part. I needed him to hold me while I wept. My heart absolutely broke for the naive twenty-one-year-old girl in the story who, after knowing him less than one week, gives her virginity away to a man who wants her to sign a domination/submission contract that will allow him to ritualistically beat her anytime he wants in the name of sexual pleasure.

The theme that runs through the book is chilling: "Wow, this older, incredibly handsome, filthy rich guy wants *me*! That must mean I'm something special!" and "Sure, he's sick and twisted, but my love will *change* him!" It actually reminded me of a girl I used to know. I still see her reflection in the mirror every morning. I'm just thankful that she looks at herself, her relationships, and sex very differently now. And I pray every day that my own twenty-year-old daughter will never experience anything remotely similar to what I did.

Whether you have read *Fifty Shades of Grey* or not is entirely beside the point. If you have chosen not to, I assure you that you will not be lost when reading *The Fantasy Fallacy*. We won't even mention anything else about the controversial series until chapter 8, mainly because we have a lot of foundational work to lay, exploring the broader topic of sexual fantasies in general before we explore BDSM in particular.

If you did read *Fifty Shades of Grey*, whether you were fascinated with it or freaked out by it, I am glad you are holding *this* book. I believe it is going to help you chew up the meat and spit out the bones when it comes to sexual fantasies. And I am praying the same prayer over you that I have prayed over myself—that God will give you eyes to view all things sexual through *His* lens and no one else's.

Go to www.ShannonEthridge.com/fantasyfallacy to find the following:

- brief summaries of each of the books in the Fifty Shades trilogy so that you can understand why some readers find the story appealing while others find it appalling
- suggestions on how to personally interact with others regarding this cultural phenomenon without offending or creating division
- an online community where you can share your thoughts about both the Fifty Shades series and *The Fantasy Fallacy*

Introduction

Reading Between the Lions

At the time of this writing, I've been alive almost forty-five years. That's 16,425 days or 394,200 hours or 23,652,000 minutes. And of those 23.6-plus million minutes, there is one minute in my history that has been incredibly pivotal, incredibly holy.

Oddly enough, I slept through that one minute. But I awoke with an unshakable "knowing" that the sixty-second dream I had experienced would have a deeply profound meaning for me for the rest of my life and perhaps for many others. If I could only be faithful to what had been entrusted to me in that dream. This book is my attempt to do just that.

It was the fall of 2011. I was snuggled beneath my goose down comforter, limbs wound tightly around my full-length body pillow, when God slipped into my slumber and brilliantly brush-stroked a cryptic message that was simply too marvelous for my own brain to have produced on its own. In this dream I was standing out in the middle of a sun-ripened, golden wheat field, wearing a flowing white dress. Perched on each side of me, one to the left and one to the right, were two majestic lions. I had my arms positioned at my sides with my hands dangling in front of their heads, as if I could be petting their manes. However, my hands weren't on their fur. My hands were in their *mouths*!

I sensed that I should be terrified that the powerful jaws of two such mighty beasts were enveloping my defenseless hands. But I noticed that I was experiencing absolutely no pain, no blood, and certainly no fear in this dream.

I did have a fleeting moment of concern that *if my hands are occupied in these two lions' mouths, then how will I ever get anything done?* Yet there seemed to be a mysterious peace blanketing me completely.

I awoke, suspecting that until I'd thoroughly analyzed and successfully deciphered this dream, there'd be no rest or satisfaction for my soul. I was right.

But what could it all mean?

A few days later I was talking on the phone. As the time approached for me to wrap up the call and get ready for bed, I was startled to recognize what I had been doing subconsciously over the past half hour. Although I don't usually do this, I had been doodling with a ballpoint pen on the back of an envelope. And what I had obliviously drawn was an embarrassingly amateur sketch of a girl . . . standing in a wheat field in a flowing white dress . . . with a lion on each side of her. And, yes, you guessed it: her hands were in the lions' mouths. No longer satisfied with disrupting my slumber, now the image was invading my waking hours too. I wasn't sure what to make of it. Perhaps it was some sort of trumpet call proclaiming my imminent epiphany.

Sometime later, I was driving down the same road I'd traveled hundreds of times before. But this time, a particular sight caught my peripheral vision, and I found myself stomping on the brakes without even thinking, craning my neck to take it in. There on someone's front porch steps were two small concrete lions, and farther back on the porch, closer to the house in the background, yet positioned directly between the two lions, was a white statue of an angel in a flowing gown. It was as if that angel and those two lions had some sort of divine power to suck the air right out of my lungs because that's exactly what the sight did to me. I sat there in the car, staring out of my window, jawbone almost touching my sternum, tears rushing into the corners of my eyes. I wanted to knock on the front door and ask if there was a story behind this configuration, but I realized that this wasn't *their* story. It was *my* story. And here it was, resurfacing once again, begging to be unraveled, longing to be understood.

I snapped a picture on my iPhone to capture the moment. It would be the first of dozens of similar photos taken. The following week I was riding my bike when suddenly what felt like a heavenly hand grabbed my head and twisted it gently to the left as if to say, *Shannon, don't miss this!* With absolute amazement I recognized that of the hundreds of houses I'd passed on that bike ride, this one had set off some sort of supernatural radar: it was decorated with, yep, lion statues.

I thought it might just be a Tyler, Texas, thing to have two lions in your front yard. I found it so odd that I'd lived in this area and driven throughout this city for almost fifteen years, yet I'd never noticed a single set of lions anywhere until after I'd had this dream. Then I saw them everywhere. And in the coming months, my stone lion radar proved amazingly accurate regardless of where I was traveling. I can take you directly to stone lions perched in places as rural as Grand Ledge, Michigan, or as metropolitan as Los Angeles, California. My spiritual GPS was guiding me to them, pointing out the soul work I had yet to do. Soon my psyche began screaming, *How long before you unravel the deeper meaning behind all of this?*

So I set about my research in every way I knew how. I combed the Internet for the symbolic meaning of lions. I began reading books on interpreting dreams. I met with two different counselors who both had some great insights. I asked certain people to pray for me and to offer any explanations that God may impress upon them.

While I can't say that I've completely solved the mystery, I will say that I've made significant progress. And I've come to believe that the dream has multiple layers of meaning. Some of those layers have been kind enough to explain themselves. Others have proven a little more shy. Or more accurately, other layers may realize that I have more growing up to do before they are ready to reveal themselves. And that's okay. I've learned to trust that God will show me whatever He wants me to know, whenever He's ready for me to know it. I'm just along for the ride, grateful to be in relationship with the God who *still* speaks to His people—sometimes through visions and dreams just as He did in the pages of Scripture, other times simply through ideas invading our brains or gut feelings.

> "Dreams are aimed at the unfinished business of your life, showing what you need to face next, what you need to learn next."[1]
> —*Robert Johnson*

For many months I focused entirely on the lions. I believed that they were the key symbols in this dream and contemplated every possible explanation I could imagine. Realizing that this was beyond the realm of my own intellectual capabilities, I pleaded with God to spell it out for me.

My next consideration was that the lions could actually represent either God or Satan. We see Jesus referred to as the "Lion from the tribe of Judah" (Rev. 5:5 NCV), but we also see Satan referred to as a "roaring lion looking for someone to devour"

(1 Peter 5:8 NIV). But as I continued to pray, neither interpretation rang entirely true.

What did ring true was that God was calling my attention to an undeniable polarity in my life coaching practice. Some of my clients beat themselves up over the least little sexual thought, feeling as if they surely had been unfaithful to their spouses and were a huge disappointment to God (neither of which was true). Others have occasionally supressed their consciences and acted out on their sexual thoughts in ways that bring incredible pain and regret later, yet they continue to feel as if they are a slave to their sexual desires (which is also untrue).

When I considered this polarity, I contemplated the position of the lions—one to my left and one to my right. I realized that the lion on the right could represent extreme right-wing thinkers, or legalists—those who beat themselves (and others) up over the smallest sexual infraction. The lion on the left could represent extreme left-wing thinkers, or liberals—those who more often turn a blind eye to their own inability to exercise sexual self-control.

I also gave careful consideration to how I have personally erred on both sides of this spectrum. There were seasons of my life, especially in my teens and early twenties, when I had an anything-goes approach to sex. Well, not *anything* but almost anything as long as it made me feel good and feel loved. (My definition of love at the time was obviously quite skewed.) There were also seasons after I had gotten my head screwed on a little straighter when I probably thought I was a little higher up on the Christian totem pole than others because of the "pure" lifestyle I was living, being so faithful to my husband and preaching to others about sexual integrity and all. I shudder at how I unintentionally but oh-so-naturally judged people for their sexual brokenness, wondering, *Why can't you get your act together like I have?* (Pretty dangerous thinking in light of how pride comes before a fall, huh?)

I realized that either of those extremes was very unhealthy. I was reminded of how we are warned to "avoid all extremes":

> *In this meaningless life of mine I have seen both of these:*
> *the righteous perishing in their righteousness,*
> *and the wicked living long in their wickedness.*
> *Do not be overrighteous,*
> *neither be overwise—*
> *why destroy yourself?*
> *Do not be overwicked,*
> *and do not be a fool—*
> *why die before your time?*
> *It is good to grasp the one*
> *and not let go of the other.*
> *Whoever fears God will avoid all extremes.* (Eccl. 7:15–18 NIV)

It was around this time that the concept for this book began crystalizing in my mind. I frequently thought about how in all things, including our sexual thoughts, we have to be careful to maintain a delicate balance between legalism and liberalism.

I'd never be legalistic enough to say that "all fantasy is evil." You'll understand why the more you read. But I'd also never be liberal enough to say, "Open your mind to whatever the heck you want!" You'll understand that, too, the further you read.

Just as the girl in the dream was standing directly in the middle of these two lions, not veering too far to the right or to the left, we have to discover our healthy sexual balance. Imagine a child standing directly atop a seesaw, one foot on one side of the fulcrum and one foot on the other. There are moments when he will need to lean his body a little more to the right to maintain balance, other times to the left. It's this constant motion, constant vigilance, constant flexibility, and constant sensitivity to which direction the Holy Spirit is guiding us in every situation that allows us to live right smack dab in the middle of God's will without stumbling and falling flat on our faces!

I know this balanced approach can be a hard concept for some to grasp. It might sound as if I'm saying, "Be a fence rider!" or "Be wishy-washy instead of staking your ground and sticking to your guns!" I'm not saying that at all. I'm merely saying we need to find and maintain a healthy balance to keep our sanity in *all* things. We don't diet religiously every single day of our lives, nor do we gorge ourselves every day. We go back and forth between feasting and fasting to maintain a healthy lifestyle. We don't pinch pennies until they bleed every day, but we don't let money sift through our hands on a daily basis either. We spend some days and save other days, hopefully saving more than we spend in the long run, but not ignoring our basic needs for the sake of hoarding money either.

The same is true with our sexual thoughts and energies. There are times when we really need to rein them in to keep from doing something stupid that will bring harm to ourselves or others. There are other times when we need to let sexual thoughts and energy flow to create the passion we all long for in marriage.

But it's more than just finding a balance and holding steady in the middle. Life is a full-participation sport. Consider a pendulum on a clock. It has to move back and forth to create energy. We can't hold it to the left or to the right or even directly in the middle. If the pendulum isn't moving back and forth constantly, it's not doing its job. The cogs of the clock won't turn, and the face won't reflect the correct time. What good is a clock that doesn't give us the correct time?

Our sexuality operates in a similar manner. In our mental and spiritual laziness, we may be tempted to find a certain mental position on certain sexual topics—fantasy, for example—and just stay there, not moving either to the right or the left *ever*! But then we lose the sexual energy we were created to produce. No! If we want our minds, bodies, and relationships to work as they're intended, there must be energy. There must be mental movement. At times, we may need to look to the God-given gift of mental fantasy to fuel our sexual passions and imaginations in marriage. Other times, we may need to reel in our thoughts to stay out of dangerous territory. Either way, whether we are intentionally opening our minds or trying to guard them, there are great benefits to peeling back the layers of our sexual thoughts to understand their deeper meanings. And once we've done so, we're better equipped to help others do the same.

As we proceed, let us remember that God is the One who created us as both spiritual and sexual beings, so He is the only One who can expose the deeper meaning that we seek. Consider me as your tour guide for this little part of your journey. I am delighted to have the opportunity to show you some of what God has shown me thus far in regard to the topic of sexual fantasy throughout these next nine chapters. You'll also glean additional insights from the "Behind the Curtain" special features and case studies. And, if needed, you can find specific resources in the back of the book that will help you overcome sexual challenges or addictions you or loved ones may be facing.

1

Why Discuss Sexual Fantasies?

After miles of wandering around in the dark, a weary traveler enters a lonely gas station. The attendant is perched on a stool behind the cash register with her eyes glued to the pages of a paperback novel.

Attempting to make his presence known, he clears his throat with great exaggeration. "Uh-huh-hum!"

"Yes?" the attendant asks, not bothering to lift her gaze.

"I'm looking for a road map," the traveler responds.

The attendant's head pops up, her brown eyes shifting all around the store to see if anyone else is hearing this conversation. With a deer-in-the-headlights look on her face, she responds directly, "No, sir. We don't carry road maps."

"Oh, well, can you tell me where another gas station is that might have one?"

Annoyed, the attendant looks up once again and replies emphatically, "You're not gonna find one around these parts."

"What do you mean? Surely there's a road map somewhere in this town that can help me figure out where I'm going!"

"Nope. Road maps don't exist for this area. And if I were you, I wouldn't go around asking for one, or else folks are going to assume you're one of *those kinds* of people."

"What do you mean, 'road maps don't exist for this area'? Surely this frequently traveled path isn't uncharted territory! And what do you mean, 'one of *those kinds* of people'? What are you talking about?" the traveler asks with great irritation.

"I mean no one is familiar enough with this region to create a road map! If you get caught asking for one, the police will know that you're one of *those people*—one who doesn't know where he's been and doesn't know where he's going! We don't allow that around here, mister, so get lost!"

"I *am* lost!" the traveler screams, quickly losing his patience. "That's why I'm *here*—asking for a road map!"

"Look, you're not going to find a road map around here! And if you ask again, I'm calling the cops!" the attendant threatens, hands on hips, eyeballs protruding out of sockets, and neck veins swelling with a combination of adrenaline and righteous indignation.

"This is ridiculous! Am I on *Candid Camera*? Am I being *Punk'd*? This can't be real!" the traveler insists.

Of course, this scenario *is* a bit on the ridiculous side. But I believe it is a pretty accurate description of what is happening inside the Christian community today. Too many folks are wandering around in a foreign land, some suspecting—but most not even realizing—that they are lost. They have no clear sense of direction. No one they can ask for a road map. Search for one and they may be labeled "one of *those kinds* of people."

The foreign land I'm referring to, of course, is this sex-saturated culture we live in, these sexually stimulated (or sexually dormant) bodies we inhabit, and these sexually motivated (or sexually frozen) minds from which we operate. With the promise of heavenly perfection, restoration, and complete redemption yet on the horizon, we are merely lost travelers here and now, trying to get our bearings and make sense of both our sexuality and our spirituality—the common denominators we all share regardless of our age, gender, race, denominational background, education level, economic status, and so on.

Trying to make perfect sense out of two such complex mysteries can feel as frustrating and fruitless as trying to brush our teeth while eating an Oreo. We all have to wonder at times:

- Where do our sexual thoughts come from?
- What do we do with them?
- Where are the mental, emotional, physical, and spiritual boundary lines?
- Can we be holy *and* horny at the same time?
- How far can we go in satisfying these overwhelming longings we sometimes feel?

Or, perhaps, a better question for some to ask is:

- If I'm a sexual being, why do I no longer experience any sexual longings at all?

GETTING OUR BEARINGS

When we have questions about sexuality, we consult the Internet, our medical dictionary, or that friend we have so much dirt on that she wouldn't possibly tell a soul we'd asked her *that* question!

Growing up, most of us never bothered consulting our parents, as they would have died of embarrassment and locked us in our rooms until we were forty. And we certainly didn't ask our spiritual leaders because we figured they probably didn't even have sex. Besides, they likely would have banned us from the church building altogether if they had found out what kinds of sexual thoughts actually go through our heads . . . even on Sundays!

If sexuality is God's invention—and it is—then we should be able to consult the church for a road map as we search for answers to our questions about all things sexual. However, if we fear that our request will be met with shock, confusion, anxiety, horror, disgust, suspicion, or judgment, perhaps even with bulging eyes and popping neck veins, then how will we navigate our way through this foreign territory? Although I can't say this of every spiritual leader or follower of Christ, I think it is safe to say that a large segment of the church seems to have no clue as to where a road map can be found. And if you ask for one, well, you must really be lost! "You must not know Jeesuuuus!" said in my most sarcastic Church Lady voice.

Can we be real for a moment? I mean, *really* real?

Even those of us who know Jesus very personally and very intimately, those of us who read our Bibles, fast frequently, tithe regularly, and pray up a storm can still feel as if we need a road map to understand our physical, spiritual, and emotional cravings! But I've got really great news. We already have such a road map *if* we're brave enough to study it.

This road map to understanding both our sexuality and our spirituality is actually composed of our deepest, most intimate personal sexual fantasies. So we'd be smart to examine such landmarks as these:

- Who are the faces in our fantasies?
- What roles do they play?
- What roles do we play?
- What primary emotions do these fantasies elicit and why?

- What event in our history created the need to experience such an emotion?
- How does this fantasy medicate emotional pain from our past or present?
- Why would humans (even Christians!) fantasize about things such as the following:
  - viewing pornography or engaging in extramarital affairs
  - bondage, domination, sadism, and masochism (as glamorized in the Fifty Shades trilogy)
  - prostitution, seduction, or rape
  - same-sex trysts, threesomes, and orgies

And the most important question to consider is this:

- Could there be an even deeper spiritual longing beneath our sexual longings?

I'll pause a moment to let you gasp for air, loosen your tie, relax your jaw, take a drink of water, and regain your composure. You may or may not be comfortable with these topics, but we *need* to discuss them. We've needed to for a l-o-n-g time. As a society, as a church, as couples and single individuals, as men and women, as parents of boys and girls struggling to make sense of their own sexuality, we need to talk about this. Ignoring the elephant in all of our living rooms certainly won't make it disappear. In fact, ignoring that elephant is causing it to mysteriously grow larger and larger.

Maybe you are just reading this book to learn how to help someone else. If so, good for you! I pray it will give you many sharp tools in your ministry or counseling tool belt. But the best way to help someone else is to help yourself first.

Before we move on with this exploration, let's pause for a quick quiz to determine just how much we understand about sexual fantasy.

TRUE OR FALSE?

T F 1. The Sexual Revolution of the past forty-plus years is all about sex.

T F 2. The church does an adequate job of teaching Christians how to appropriately assess and discuss the topic of sexual fantasy.

T F 3. All fantasy is inappropriate, unhealthy, and sinful.

T F 4. Sexual fantasy and lust are the same thing.

T F 5. Christians control their sexual thoughts and actions better than others.

T F 6. Sexual fantasies provide a road map to the sexual fulfillment we crave.

T F 7. Sexual fantasies are better left unspoken and unexplored.

T F 8. Sexual fantasy is really just the brain's way of driving us to do evil things.

T F 9. Anxiety, confusion, or fear over sexual fantasies is not a common issue.

T F 10. Interpreting sexual fantasies isn't going to solve any of the world's problems.

Now let's see how you did!

1. The Sexual Revolution of the past forty-plus years is all about sex. *False.*

The Sexual Revolution actually isn't about sex at all. It's about broken people using other people, desperately trying to medicate their own emotional pain through sexual acts. It's about loneliness, isolation, rejection, insecurities, codependency, boredom, and selfishness.

God's intention for sexual intimacy is to provide a wonderful way for two people—forever committed to one another in a marriage relationship—to *give* to one another through intense pleasure, passion, affirmation, tenderness, mutual trust, and mutual euphoria. Just think of what the world would be like if we were to experience *that* kind of constructive sexual revolution instead of the destructive one we have experienced!

2. The church does an adequate job of teaching Christians how to appropriately assess and discuss the topic of sexual fantasy. *False.*

I don't know about you, but I've never heard a single sermon on the roles, the rules, the benefits, or the boundaries of sexual fantasy. Perhaps the reason is that the word *fantasy* doesn't appear in the Bible at all, at least not in the several translations I consulted.

The whole topic can be extremely difficult to discuss simply because of our lack of understanding. For example, I recently heard from a gentleman who was quite unhappy with me for addressing the topic of sexual fantasy in my most recent book, *The Sexually Confident Wife.* We exchanged several cordial e-mails back and forth before I finally thought to ask the question, "If I had used the term sexual *thoughts* instead of *fantasies,* would you feel any differently about what I had to say on the topic?"

After a few hours of contemplation, he replied that indeed, we *all* have sexual thoughts, and that's a perfectly appropriate thing to discuss. So then I posed the question, "Can you explain to me your perceived difference between a *sexual thought* and a *sexual fantasy*?"

Through continued e-mail exchanges, we together considered the following:

- Is it a matter of the *content* of the thought?
- Is it how the thought makes you feel in response?
- Is it a matter of how many seconds it stays in your head? Perhaps less than two seconds flat and it's merely a thought, but anything more than 2.1 seconds becomes a fantasy?

We both had to laugh at how difficult it is for Christians to have a clear conversation when we don't even have a clear vocabulary for the topic! So let's establish some definitions before we go any further.

Since the Bible doesn't specifically mention fantasy, let's consult the dictionary. Dictionary.com defines the word *fantasy* as:

1. imagination, especially when extravagant and unrestrained.
2. the forming of mental images, especially wondrous or strange fancies; imaginative conceptualizing.
3. a mental image, especially when unreal or fantastic; vision: *a nightmare fantasy.*
4. *Psychology.* an imagined or conjured up sequence fulfilling a psychological need; daydream.
5. a hallucination.[1]

For the purposes of our discussion, I'm going to lean toward the fourth definition—that sexual fantasies are imaginative thoughts that fulfill some sort of psychological need. I believe examining the fantasy for the purpose of discerning the underlying psychological need is absolutely key to helping us control those fantasies before they control us!

3. All fantasy is inappropriate, unhealthy, and sinful. ***False.***

From the time we are small children, we are encouraged by our parents and by society to fantasize. "What do you want to be when you grow up?" is one of the most common questions asked of a young child. How else are they to know if they don't daydream about different roles they could play in society? In this context, fantasy is healthy and even vital to growth.

Consider that. . .

- to fantasize about where to go to college and what to study means that we are intelligent.
- to fantasize about getting more out of our careers means that we are ambitious.
- to fantasize about getting physically fit means that we are health conscious.
- to fantasize about getting more out of our sex lives, well, that means we must be lustful, perverted, sick, and twisted.

Of course, that last statement is simply not true. It is normal and healthy to want the most out of our sex lives, and sometimes fantasy *is* the best way to achieve that goal—to envision what you might find pleasurable and especially to envision what kind of pleasurable acts you would enjoy offering to your spouse.

As I was discussing this book idea with respected friends and colleagues, one of the most common questions I heard was, "Do you think *all* fantasy is wrong?" Let me state my position up front. I absolutely do not think that *all* fantasy is wrong, but those fantasies that push beyond what is socially or spiritually acceptable are most often rooted in childhood trauma or unresolved pain. The goal of this book isn't to judge whether fantasies are "right or wrong" but, rather, to help people examine sexual fantasies, recognize their roots, and invite God to help them heal their pain.

4. Sexual fantasy and lust are the same thing. ***False.***

Now that we have established a definition for sexual fantasy, let's talk about lust. Any time the word *lust* is mentioned in the Bible, it is in reference to craving something that doesn't belong to the person doing the lusting, such as to "lust after [other] gods" (Exod. 34:15 NLT), "give up your lust for money" (Job 22:24 NLT), or "not to look with lust at a young woman" or "neighbor's wife" (Job 31:1, 9 NLT).

Lust is never mentioned in the context of a marriage partner wanting to please or be pleased by their spouses. Such desire isn't lust at all. As we are told in 1 Corinthians 7:9 (NLT), "It's better to marry than to burn with lust." In other words, the act of marriage transforms our lustful longings (to have sex with someone we are not yet married to) into longings that are holy, pure, and unequivocally right because marriage is God's ordained place for those passionate and pleasurable longings to be fully explored and enjoyed. (Of course, there are instances where people begin selfishly using and abusing their marriage partner sexually, so lust is possible in marriage.)

In his book *The Bondage Breaker,* Neil T. Anderson provides even more insight. He shows that while our sexual thoughts and desires are perfectly normal, they can begin to cross a line. He writes:

> Sex is a God-given part of our autonomic nervous system. Normal sexual functioning is a regular, rhythmic part of life. But when Jesus said, "Everyone who looks on a woman to lust for her has committed adultery with her already in his heart" (Matthew 5:28), He was describing something beyond the boundary of God's design for sex. The word for lust is *epithumos.*

> The prefix *epi* means "to add to," signifying that something is being added to a normal drive. Jesus challenged us not to add onto the God-given sexual drive by polluting our minds with lustful thoughts. The only way to control your sex life is to control your thought life.[2]

Unfortunately, controlling your thought life is much easier said than done, but I pray this book will help you do just that—by helping you understand (rather than ignore) the sexual thoughts that often surface in your mind.

Another reason I don't think sexual fantasy and lust are the same thing is that many coaching clients tell me that their sexual fantasies often include something they don't desire at all. A man who fantasizes (or has a sexual thought) about being with another man often finds the thought rather repulsive, yet it can resurface time and time again. A woman who fantasizes (or who has an occasional sexual thought) about being raped doesn't really want to be raped. So for the purposes of discussion, not all fantasies can be classified as lustful thoughts. Sexual fantasies are merely thoughts that may be trying to tell us something our minds are not consciously aware of. There is no need to shoot the messengers.

5. Christians control their sexual thoughts and actions better than others. *False.*

While the answer to this question probably *should* be true in light of the amazing power we have available to us to resist temptation, I think we have to admit that the answer is all too often *false*. Christians struggle, just as much as anyone else, with sexual sin, which includes premarital sex, extramarital sex, and pornography usage.

In talking last year with the manager of one Cincinnati hotel, part of a chain that hosts some of the largest Christian conventions in our nation, I discovered that the hotel chain profits greatly from hosting these particular meetings. The conventions are attended each year by hordes of pastors, religious broadcasters, Christian writers, speakers, and musicians. Would you like to guess what is attributed to the hotel's bottom-line increase during these conferences? According to the manager, purchases of pornographic movies are tremendous!

It is time to stop pretending that Christians don't struggle with sexual sin. It is easy to see the news and assume that only the most powerful politicians or famous celebrities run the risk of acting out their fantasies in dangerous and destructive ways. But surely "real" people don't act that way! Especially not "real Christians," right?

Wrong. My life coaching practice has been composed almost exclusively of Christian women and men who appear very "normal" on the outside. However, as they have given me glimpses into what is going on with them on the inside, it has been heartbreaking to see how their sexual fantasies have led them down some very painful paths, often because they chose to act them out. You will read case studies of many of these clients sprinkled throughout this book.[3]

6. Sexual fantasies provide a road map to the sexual fulfillment we crave. *False.*

It is easy to assume that fantasies must be a road map to future fulfillment. If __________ is what I think about, dream about, fantasize about, well, it must be *what I want*! If it feels that good in the fantasy, I can only imagine how good it's going to feel in reality!

Yet many have learned (some the hard way) that most fantasies are better left as fantasy—*not* reality. In fact, some of the fantasizing we do is merely to medicate the emotional pain we have caused ourselves by acting out on *previous* fantasies. What a vicious cycle. As they say in the recovery movement, "The definition of insanity is trying the same thing over and over, expecting different results this time."

This reminds me of a Richard Torregrossa cartoon I saw in Robin Norwood's book *Daily Meditations for Women Who Love Too Much.* In the cartoon, a woman is on her hands and knees on the sidewalk underneath a streetlight at night. A police officer approaches and asks, "What are you looking for?"

"My keys," the woman replies.

"Is this where you lost them?" the officer insightfully inquires.

The woman responds, "No, but it's the only place I can see to look."

Sometimes we think our sexual fantasies are the only places we can find the fulfillment we crave because they are the only places we can see to look, but sexual fantasies are not accurate road maps for discovering what we want in the present or future. They are, however, excellent road maps into the past.

Why would we want to go *there*? So that we can recognize and heal the unresolved pain that often drives us to do some pretty stupid things. Only then can we fully integrate our sexual fantasies and our Christian faith to become the women, men, wives, husbands, moms, and dads God created us to be.

7. Sexual fantasies are better left unspoken and unexplored. *False.*

Granted, certain individuals have tried to openly share some of their most troubling sexual fantasies only to face harsh consequences, such as:

- Olivia, who was asked to resign her position as a Sunday school teacher when she confessed to her pastor's wife that she struggled with sexual fantasy and masturbation.
- Kent, whose wife packed her bags and left him when he

admitted that he was having a hard time controlling his thoughts about a woman at work.

- Marcia, who admitted to a female friend that she was hooked on lesbian pornography, only to have that female friend encourage her to give lesbianism a try, which produced even more feelings of guilt and shame.

We always run a risk when we choose to be vulnerable about anything sexual. And sometimes it really *is* better to keep certain things to ourselves . . . at least until we find someone who can truly help us without hurting us first.

But when we do find that person who can help us see beyond the trees and into the forest, the healing it can bring is astounding! And becoming a "safe person" who can help others experience the sexual and spiritual breakthroughs they are looking for is even more rewarding.

Therefore, I'm going to urge you throughout this book not to ignore your own fantasies but to carefully consider their deeper meanings. If we look beyond the fantasies themselves, we can expose the driving forces operating within us that often lead us toward destructive relational patterns. This deeper understanding of ourselves and how we relate with others is an invaluable part of growing, maturing, and finding freedom to fully enjoy our sexuality.

8. Sexual fantasy is really just the brain's way of driving us to do evil things. *False.*

I have a dear friend and mentor, Jarratt Major, who is an eighty-year-old licensed marriage-and-family therapist and a retired minister. I have been meeting monthly with him and two other professional counselors for almost four years now, in a group we affectionately refer to as "Shrink Rap," so called because we are a bunch of shrinks who rap about our own life journeys. Jarratt, considered the padre of the group, has taught us two incredibly valuable nuggets of wisdom that have shaped my thinking and sparked my imagination to write this book:

1. Fantasies are really just the brain's way of trying to heal itself.
2. If you don't learn to face your fantasies, they may bite you on the butt as you're trying to run away from them![4]

Grasping these principles has transformed my thought life, enhanced my self-esteem, and even saved my marriage. For example, many years ago, each time a man turned my head I'd panic. *Is this destiny's way of telling me I married the wrong person? Is this the beginning of the end of my marriage? Is an extramarital affair inevitable here?* These were the questions I would naively wonder.

Fortunately my husband was always far more understanding of temptations and fantasies than I was. As I tearfully confessed my thoughts and asked him for forgiveness and to hold me accountable, he would often remind me, "Shannon, this is not about you and me. This is about you and your dad."

This notion has made a lot more sense in light of the two principles Jarratt has shared with me. These fantasies of other, usually older men were really just my brain's way of trying to heal the hurts of feeling so emotionally distanced from a father who simply didn't know what to do with a daughter. If I ignored the pain that produced the fantasies, I could have easily fallen into those affairs. Instead, I faced the pain, going through months of intense group and individual therapy to deal with my "daddy issues."

Now, after forty-five years of life and almost twenty-three years of marriage, I have learned that when my head gets turned and my heart feels drawn toward another man, I don't need to panic or run to confession. Instead, I'll approach Greg and ask, "Would you mind holding me like a baby?" As my six-foot-seven husband scoops me up in his arms, I'm reminded that I have all the love I need—all I can handle—wrapped up in this relationship called marriage. But even if I didn't have a husband at all, the love of my heavenly Father envelops me enough to keep me safe from my own sexual fantasies if I will choose to bask in His presence rather than run toward the object of my fantasy.

Therefore, the question to ask ourselves is never, "How can I fulfill this fantasy?" or even "How can I ignore this fantasy?" but "What can I learn from this fantasy?" and "How can I heal this pain that is causing me to fantasize in this direction in the first place?" Like an alchemist who extracts gold from base metals, we can extract some of the most valuable nuggets of wisdom from the most base of our mental inventory.

9. Anxiety, confusion, or fear over sexual fantasies is not a common issue. *False.*

Research shows that 84 percent of men and 67 percent of women have sexual fantasies, so I think it's safe to say that on average, approximately three out of four people have them.[5] While I've not found a study reporting what percentage of those individuals wrestle with negative feelings about their fantasies, I'd have to guess it is a pretty significant population based on the number of people we hear from each week at www.ShannonEthridge.com, submitting prayer requests such as:

> I want to be delivered from sexual fantasies about TV characters. I would love to have a healthy, wonderful relationship with a "real" man that God would love for me to be with. I don't feel like there is anyone to share this with, so I would like your prayer partners to pray for me. —Jill

I am really struggling with purity. I realize that the only time I really get into sex with my husband is when I fantasize. I crave sex more than he does and am just having a hard time keeping my mind pure. I don't even know where to begin. I am rereading your book *Every Woman's Battle* because I haven't read it in years, and I know I need some encouragement in this area. Thanks for your prayers. —Katy

My wife is the only child of an alcoholic mother and was raised in a very strict church environment. She has a lot of emotional issues (anger, depression, major mood swings) that make it very difficult for me to feel connected to her sexually. As a result of all of this, I find myself fantasizing like crazy about other women—what they'd be willing to do in bed and the fun we could have together. I know this is dangerous. I just don't know how to control it. I've prayed until I'm blue in the face, so I guess I'm just asking for others to join me in prayer, both for my wife and for me to keep my mind from going places where I know it shouldn't. —Michael

I am happily married to a wonderful man, but I have a huge crush on my married realtor. I have confided in a few godly girlfriends, and they are praying and holding me accountable. Every time I fantasize about him I regret it and pray and confess, yet I keep slipping back. I can't seem to take my thoughts captive! I love my husband, our marriage is good, and I am attracted to him. The only thing I can think of that I am getting out of this crush is the ego boost or rush of imagining a new and different man finding me attractive. Our house sale closes soon, but I am worried that I will hang on to my fantasy version of this man for some time. And that if I can't figure out how to control this crush, a different one may come along in the future

> and be more dangerous. What if I develop a crush on someone I actually know personally rather than a temporary professional in my life!?!?!? I need to let this guy go in my mind and heart before it damages my marriage. Please pray for me. —Sheryl

If you are a counselor, spiritual leader, or just a friend with a good listening ear, perhaps you are hearing similar pleas. My prayer is that this book can be a reliable compass for you to guide hurting people toward helpful answers and hopeful solutions.

10. Interpreting sexual fantasies isn't going to solve any of the world's problems. *False.*

Consider for a moment some of the biggest relational problems facing society today:

- Marriages that don't make it
- Families that fall apart
- Children who are caught in the middle and grow up with all kinds of emotional baggage as a result
- The financial pressures of single parenting
- The resulting burdens on our nation's education and welfare systems
- People who suffer in silence or who look to drugs, alcohol, sex, or anything to numb their pain

The list could go on and on.

There are several possible origins for these difficulties, but often individuals, marriages, and families are breaking down because of unresolved sexual issues. And where do these sexual issues begin? In the human mind. Any sexually charged or relationally destructive words that we have ever spoken, any commitments that we have made or broken, any fantasies that we have conjured up or managed to control—all of these things flow out of the fascinating human brain. And like any other bodily organ, the brain's main quest is to heal itself from any emotional damage it has experienced in the past.

> "What is most hidden in us is also what is most universal. *Everyone* has secrets that need to be uncovered and healed, and as we face our own, we help create a climate in which others can do the same. As we work on our own healing, we help bring about healing in the world."[6]
> *—Robin Norwood*

So won't you join me on this healing journey into the deepest recesses of the sexual mind? Perhaps we'll discover that our sexual fantasies don't have to be a big stumbling block that trips us up. They don't have to send shock waves and painful ripple effects into our families for generations to come. They may actually be more like priceless pearls of wisdom underneath the mounds of mattresses that have been suffocating our society for far too long. And maybe exposing the deeper meaning behind sexual thoughts will remove and redeem these pearls, bringing us the relational peace and rest our minds and marriages long for.

BEHIND THE CURTAIN: HOW IS FANTASY A FRIEND?

Just the word itself—*fantasy*—can elicit all kinds of anxiety among Christians. In fact, *fantasy* seems to be an even more taboo word than *sex*! But before we throw the baby out with the bathwater and assume that all fantasy is unhealthy, dangerous, and therefore entirely off limits, let's consider how fantasy can actually be a friend.

1. **Fantasy can help numb us to unbearable pain.**
   When my daughter was a brand-new driver, she hit a tree and did a face-plant into her windshield, requiring twelve stitches to keep her ear attached to her head. As she lay trembling on the emergency room table wide-eyed with fright, I was desperate to help her cope with the pain and trauma of it all. I resorted to fantasy. "Erin, let's pretend we're going on a trip to anywhere in the world you want to go! Where to? Australia? Okay! Now tell me who do you want to take with you? Our friends Terrica and Sharon? Absolutely! Who else? Where will you want to take them once we arrive? What will we do there?" The fantasy went on for twenty minutes—long enough for the doctor to finish his sewing project. Through this experience, I was reminded of how our imagination is a gift from God—one that can distract us from great pain when necessary.

2. **Fantasy can motivate us toward an established goal.**
   Amy just lost sixty pounds and feels better (and sexier) than she has in decades. When I asked her how she did it, I expected she'd tell me about an intense workout routine or a special diet she followed. But to my surprise, she replied, "I fantasized my way to my weight loss goal! I just kept imagining at every meal what I'd love to look like by my fiftieth birthday, and I naturally ate less!"

3. **Fantasy can help us prepare for a life transition.**
   Cassie came to me incredibly concerned about whether she should ever get married because the idea of sex was so scary and repulsive to her. In her late twenties, she still experienced such sexual anxiety that she asked, "If I do get married, can I ask him to cut 'those things' off?" I inquired

what "things" she was referring to and learned that she grew physically ill over the thought of a man's testicles "bumping up against her" during intercourse. I assured her that *no man* would ever be willing to do that—not even for his wife—and that when she fell in love, she'd never dream of asking that wonderful man to castrate himself! Indeed, Cassie eventually fell in love and got engaged, but she was still very nervous about the honeymoon (and every night thereafter). So she began preparing herself mentally through the use of fantasy. She envisioned repeatedly that she would enjoy her husband's body, and vice versa, in very holy and healthy ways, and that there would be absolutely no feelings of anxiety or disgust with any particular body part. After the wedding Cassie proudly proclaimed, "Our honeymoon rocked! Nothing really freaked me out at all, thanks to the mental exercises you recommended!"

4. **Fantasy can warn us about a possible future event.** Janie set up a coaching session thinking she'd crossed a horrible line. She was distracted almost daily by thoughts that a particular tall, dark, and handsome stranger may board the train she rode home on. She'd seen him a handful of times but had never interacted with him at all. When I asked what line she had crossed, she admitted to having fantasies that this man might engage her in conversation and that their "accidental tourist" relationship would blossom into a sexual affair. "Is that what you want?" I inquired; she responded with shock and horror. "So if it's *not* what you want, could it be that the purpose of the fantasy is simply to warn you that this possibility exists and to encourage you to rehearse an appropriate response?" A

few weeks later, this stranger's spotlight was indeed aimed in Janie's direction. However, by delivering the exact response she'd been rehearsing, Janie was able to nip a potentially inappropriate relationship in the bud.

5. **Fantasy can help us endure separation.**
   When I speak to military wives, I am always asked the question, "Is it okay for me to fantasize about sex with my husband while he's deployed?" I usually grab that woman by the shoulders, give her a playful shake, and declare, "You'd better!" Seriously, how could military spouses (both husbands and wives) cope with such a lengthy, painful, and scary separation from one another if they felt sinful entertaining sexual thoughts of one another? There is nothing sinful about healthy sexual thoughts of your marriage partner—*ever*—even if your spouse is gone to the grocery store for only an hour. But for spouses who have to endure an extended separation, sexual fantasy can keep the home fires burning until a passionate sexual reunion is possible.

6. **Fantasy can comfort us as we age.**
   When I made the announcement on my blog that I was writing this book, I received an e-mail from an anonymous man. He explained, "As we grow older, I enjoy letting my mind wander back to the good old days—back to when my wife would let me boldly stare at her youthful, beautiful body, when we had all the strength and energy required for frequent afternoon delights and weekend sexual marathons, back to when I wasn't concerned about whether I could maintain an erection until I'd crossed the finish line. Recalling these wonderful times we've shared

together keeps me from looking at pornography or lusting over other women—(I'm old, but I'm not dead)—so I think fantasy can serve a good purpose."

Indeed, fantasy can serve *many* good purposes, so don't knock it completely until you try it.

2

The Benefits of Boundaries

One of my fondest memories from childhood is playing badminton with my older brother. Next to our house was a vacant lot with towering pecan trees spaced perfectly to support a badminton net, so many hours were spent gleefully lobbing birdies back and forth from one side of our makeshift court to the other.

However, my brother liked to win, and his perception of the boundary lines seemed a little different than mine. If I let a birdie drop on my side of the court anywhere near the boundary line, he'd insist that it was "in bounds" and therefore his point. But when he let a birdie drop to the ground anywhere close to the boundary line on his side of the court, he'd insist he did it on purpose because it was "out-of-bounds."

I found it maddening but played along just to enjoy his company because that's what little sisters do. But had we spray-painted clearer boundary lines along the grass in that vacant lot, I would have won more games or at least scored a few more points than I received credit for.

Having clearer boundary lines helps in most situations, and tackling this subject of sexual fantasy is no different. As I have been sharing this vision with many friends and colleagues, the question I seem to receive most is: *Where will you draw the line?* Or as one Facebook friend asked: *How do you face your fantasies without acting out on them?*

So before we venture much further, let's discuss a few different spectrums and classifications so that we can determine what types of activities should be considered out-of-bounds and establish a designated safe playing space for our mental sexual activities. Here are some helpful tools for our discussion:

- The Psychology/Theology Spectrum
- The Repression/Expression Spectrum
- Three Types of Sexual Fantasy

THE PSYCHOLOGY/THEOLOGY SPECTRUM

It seems that what we learn in psychology class and what we might learn in Sunday school about the topic of sexual fantasy are miles apart. And perhaps you have already wondered, "Which approach does Shannon take to sexual fantasy? A psychological one? Or a theological one?"

May I ask in response, Why does it have to be an either/or question? Why can't it be a both/and question? In other words, isn't it possible to embrace *both* a psychological *and* a theological perspective on sexual fantasy?

I believe that we can and that we are wise to do so. After completing a master's degree in counseling and human relationships from Liberty University and completing certification as a life coach through the American Association of Christian Counselors,

I have learned that psychology and theology do not always contradict one another!

First, let's consider what psychology says about fantasies. Here are just a couple of examples, taken from my human sexuality textbook from Liberty University:

> Fantasy is a safe way to experience a sexual activity that a person might not morally, safely, legally, or maybe physically, be able to do in real life. The only limit is your imagination.[1]

> Because they allow us to indulge our impulses without social constraints or conventions, sexual fantasies provide an interesting window to our evolutionary instincts.[2]

For the Christian man or woman, this perspective can sound scary at first glance, as if it goes completely against what we're taught in Scripture. However, the same textbook also says:

> Acting out a fantasy [can be] cause for concern if it involves pressuring or coercing an unwilling partner, *goes against your value system*, or puts you or a partner at physical or *emotional risk*.[3] (italics mine)

> . . . you can control the content of the fantasy with deliberate scripting, editing, and casting.[4]

In other words, some psychologists take into consideration that if certain sexual fantasies create spiritual guilt or inner turmoil for an individual, that's a bad thing. And most psychologists acknowledge that we do not have to let fantasies control us. We are mentally capable of controlling them, which is also what the

Bible encourages us to do. So let's shift to the other end of the spectrum and consider what the Bible has to say about our thoughts. These passages in particular come to mind:

> You have heard that it was said, "You must not be guilty of adultery." But I tell you that if anyone looks at a woman and wants to sin sexually with her, in his mind he has already done that sin with the woman. If your right eye causes you to sin, take it out and throw it away. It is better to lose one part of your body than to have your whole body thrown into hell. (Matt. 5:27–29 NCV)

> Surely you know that the people who do wrong will not inherit God's kingdom. Do not be fooled. Those who sin sexually, worship idols, take part in adultery, those who are male prostitutes, or men who have sexual relations with other men, those who steal, are greedy, get drunk, lie about others, or rob—these people will not inherit God's kingdom. (1 Cor. 6:9–10 NCV)

At first glance these passages can be even scarier than what psychology teaches. That we're *not* going to heaven if we sin sexually? That we sin sexually simply by looking at someone lustfully? That we are to gouge out our eyes if they cause us to lust? *Gee whiz!* No wonder many abandon Christianity because they feel as if they'll never measure up to such unrealistic standards.

But let's press the Pause button and investigate these scriptures a little further to fully understand the bigger picture of what Jesus and Paul were saying. My pastor, Doug Clark of Grace Community Church in Tyler, Texas, recently preached a sermon on these two passages, and they helped me make more sense out of them than ever before.

Regarding the Matthew 5 text, Doug pointed out that Jesus was addressing the Pharisees' notion that they were "holy enough" to get themselves into heaven. This was ridiculous, of course, because only Jesus fits that category. We need *Him* and the blood He shed for us on the cross to gain entry into heaven. So in order to dispel the myth in the Pharisees' minds that *their* righteousness, particularly their own sexual purity, was enough to earn salvation, Jesus used the illustration of looking upon a woman lustfully and told how they had already committed adultery with her in their hearts and minds once they'd done so (Matt. 5:28). Jesus could have said, in other words, "Hey, guys! That little thing that you do so often—practically every day, without even noticing—thinking that it's not hurting anyone or that it's completely inconsequential, that little thing is enough to disqualify you. There's no way you are holy enough to gain God's approval. You need *Me* to get you into heaven!"

Of course Jesus went on to explain that this "little thing" isn't so little in His rule book. He said, "Gouge out your eye if it causes you to sin!" (Matt. 5:29, author's paraphrase) Are we to take Him literally? If we did, the entire church would be walking around blind yet *still* lusting in our hearts and minds because of the fallen state we live in. Physical blindness wouldn't be sufficient to cure us of all our sexual depravity.

No, Jesus was using strong language to make His point: we are to take sin seriously. Taking lustful thoughts seriously is reason number 101 why I'm writing this book.

Reading 1 Corinthians 6:9–10, particularly the part about the sexually immoral not inheriting the kingdom of God, it's easy to assume that sexual purity is a salvation matter. I want to declare that this is *not* my understanding of Scripture. Just as Jesus said to the Pharisees, "Your sexual purity does not *qualify* you for heaven," we can also assume the reverse to be true. "Your sexual impurity does not *disqualify* you from heaven either."

In this passage Paul was addressing *believers* in Christ who were saved yet continued to act like those who *weren't believers* or those indulging in all kinds of selfish sins because they weren't saved or sanctified. Paul wasn't saying to believers, "If you do this, you're scratched off heaven's reception list!" He was saying, "Because you *are* on the reception list of invitees, you should not act like those who aren't!"

So again, I want to make it clear that salvation is not a matter of sexual purity, but strictly a matter of trusting in Christ as your personal Savior. However, sexual purity *is* (or should be) a natural by-product of being sanctified, which means becoming more holy simply because we are in close relationship with the Holy Spirit.

How can we do that—be made more holy—while walking around in these sexual bodies, thinking these sexual thoughts, and wrestling with these sexual fantasies and urges? By adopting Paul's strategy for victory in any spiritual battle we face:

> We do live in the world, but we do not fight in the same way the world fights. We fight with weapons that are different from those the world uses. Our weapons have power from God that can destroy the enemy's strong places. We destroy people's arguments and every proud thing that raises itself against the knowledge of God. We capture every thought and make it give up and obey Christ. (2 Cor. 10:3–6 NCV)

Did you catch that? With God's help, we are able to capture *every thought* and make it *obedient* to Christ. We are able to operate completely within our value system, reduce our emotional risk, and control the content of our fantasies with deliberate scripting, editing, and casting, just as psychology supports.

So perhaps psychology and theology aren't so very far apart after all! With that in mind, let's move on to discuss what we are to do with our sexual urges when they arise.

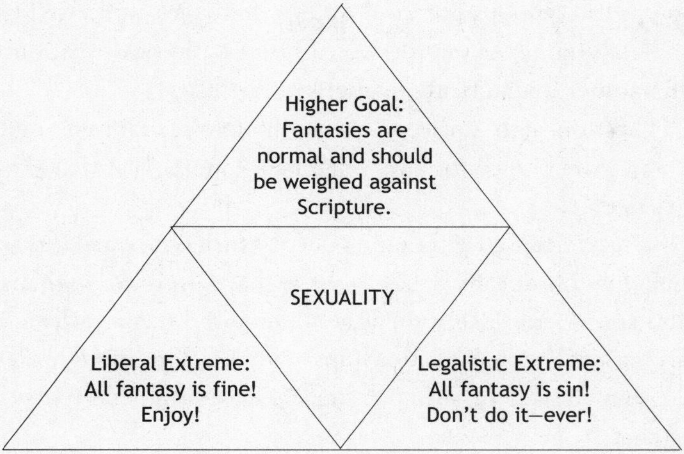

THE REPRESSION/EXPRESSION SPECTRUM

After I finish a speaking engagement, I'm occasionally approached by a few attending the event, wanting to talk. It doesn't take long before I realize they're wondering the same thing that many others do. "Where is the switch? Can I just turn off the 'sexuality switch' so that I don't have to wrestle with these temptations any longer?" Sure, it might seem much easier if such a switch existed. Unfortunately, it doesn't. As long as we are living and breathing, we are sexual beings. From the cradle to the grave, we simply can't escape this reality.

However, some people still try, and some might even succeed to a large degree, but at what cost? This denial of all sexual thoughts and feelings is called repression. Dictionary.com defines *repression* as "the rejection from consciousness of painful or disagreeable ideas, memories, feelings, or impulses."[5] In other words, repression occurs when you do not let yourself experience any sexual thoughts or feelings to any degree. Unfortunately repressing all sexual desires doesn't work. (I can just hear Dr. Phil asking,

"How is *that* working for you?") Or it works *too* well, leaving us completely numb to *any* desire to be in a physical relationship with another sexual being (namely, our spouses).

That's too high a price to pay; complete sexual repression is not a healthy choice for any individual, especially if that person is married.

But just because we shouldn't or can't turn our sexual thoughts completely off doesn't mean we have the right to leave them on at full speed, expressing them at whim and drawing others into dysfunctional sexual relationships with us. The Bible makes it clear that the act of sexual intimacy was designed strictly for marriage.

If we are not married, we are still *sexual* beings. We are simply not sexually *active*. At least that's how it is supposed to work according to God's perfect plan. So an alternative to sexual repression for single people is sublimation, defined as "the diversion of the energy of a sexual or other biological impulse from its immediate goal to one of a more acceptable social, moral, or aesthetic nature or use."[6] In other words, instead of looking at pornography and masturbating or pursuing a willing partner with your sexual energies, channel that same energy into painting, writing, dancing, singing, or some other healthy pursuit or hobby. Some of the greatest works of art, books, and songs have been birthed simply because their originator was sublimating sexual passions rather than expressing them.

When I think of sexual repression and expression, I think of a giant red beach ball being forced to the bottom of a pool. The main problem is that it won't stay there unless you are incredibly vigilant and keep something heavy perched directly on top of it. The second that it is not being forced down with ample weight, it is going to come rocketing not just to the surface but right out of the water.

Think of some of the most infamous sex scandals of our day involving Christians, and this "beach ball" effect has probably manifested itself in those relationships. When sexual desires were ignored and repressed for a long period of time, the moment vigilance waned these desires rose to the surface with great force (and painful consequences). They were suddenly and forcefully expressed instead of repressed.

A more effective approach to properly managing a beach ball would be to simply let it float naturally on top of the water without tension to go in either direction—up or down, unnatural repression or unhealthy expression. Then it won't have to fight against such a strong gravitational force, nor will it suddenly soar to scary heights when released. It just floats there calmly and serenely, not causing any harm to anyone.

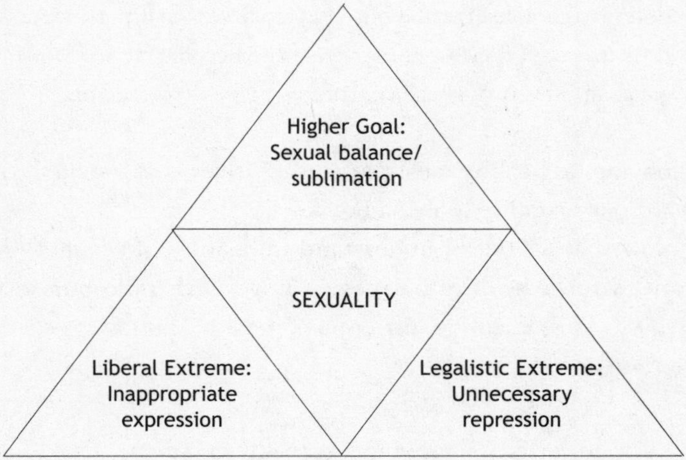

If we can accept the fact that a beach ball is best managed by simply letting it float naturally on top of the water, can't we also accept the fact that there is a healthy middle ground to managing our own sexual desires? A balance where we're neither expressing nor repressing unholy desires, but accepting the sexual nature of our own humanity, sublimating sexual desires when necessary, and resting in God's grace to keep us directly in the center of God's will? That's certainly the goal.

Gary Thomas, author of *Sacred Marriage*, affirms that a healthy sexual balance means allowing ourselves to live in this tension between repressing and expressing our sexual desires. He states:

> Sometimes dam managers opt to let the water flow rather freely; other times they hold it down to a trickle.
>
> That's what marriage teaches us to do. Sometimes it is healthy and good to let marital passions run free, even if we fear that we are almost crossing the line over into lust. Some people make the mistake of believing that because they have been burned by their passion and their sexual hunger, the antidote is to completely cut it off. They do to sex what an anorexic does to food: I don't want to overeat and become fat, so I won't eat at all. This isn't a healthy attitude—it's a demented one.[7]

Having a healthy attitude, rather than a demented one, toward our sexuality is absolutely key!

Now that we better understand the nature of sexuality and the need for a healthy balance in how we handle our sexual energies, let's examine different kinds of fantasies we can experience.

THREE TYPES OF SEXUAL FANTASY

As a result of some very interesting conversations with a few counseling professionals, in particular Chris Legg, LPC, I'd like to propose that there are three words that best describe the various types of sexual thoughts:

- *Autoerotic*—automatically "produces sexual excitement or pleasure without association with another person or intentional external stimulation"[8]
- *Erotic*—intending to arouse or satisfy "sexual desire"[9] within marriage through an activity that is perfectly acceptable to both spouses and not expressly forbidden in Scripture
- *Illicit*—"disapproved of or not permitted for moral or ethical reasons,"[10] mainly due to the relational context of the participants not being married to one another

Autoerotic Thoughts

Applying these definitions directly to our sexual fantasies, *autoerotic* fantasies include sexual thoughts that come into our brains completely unbidden. In other words, we didn't conjure them up by looking at pornography or reading a romance novel. The thought simply came to us—out of the blue—either in our dreams or our random thoughts.

Should we feel guilty for autoerotic thoughts, dreams, or fantasies? Many do, but there's absolutely no reason to beat ourselves up over what happens naturally in our human bodies, even if those thoughts "turn us on" sexually. We can simply choose not to act on them. I believe this is what it means to take a thought captive and make it obedient to Christ (2 Cor. 10:5).

Based on some research that I stumbled upon recently, it would be impossible for humans not to be turned on by random autoerotic thoughts. There are several nerves that run directly from the genitals to our brains, so thoughts that cause the sexual parts of our brains to light up are also going to light up our loins! And any sensations to our genitals whatsoever can trigger these nerves to send sexy messages to the brain. In other words, we couldn't turn off all sexual thoughts if we tried, unless, of course, we severed this bundle of nerves altogether.[11]

So let's do ourselves a favor and give up the guilt over *all* sexual thought. It's simply unrealistic to expect this of ourselves, like expecting elephants to give up *all* thoughts of peanuts or monkeys to give up *all* thoughts of bananas. Not gonna happen.

Erotic Thoughts

The next category is *erotic* thoughts, the goal of which is to intentionally arouse ourselves or our partners. For a single person, intentionally entertaining erotic fantasy is like playing with fire and is perhaps why Song of Solomon warns, "Do not arouse or awaken love" before it is time (2:7; 3:5; 8:4 NIV).

But if you are married, of course, intentionally arousing yourself and your spouse is a good thing. I am reminded of a seventy-two-year-old woman who called me in response to my book *The Sexually Confident Wife* a few years ago. She explained that for the first thirty years of her marriage, she was sexually frozen. She didn't want to entertain her husband's sexual advances at all because she feared displeasing God with the thoughts that ran through her mind when having sex. You can imagine the impact this mind-set had on their marriage. Divorce court was the next scheduled stop in their relational journey, until her husband convinced her to see a therapist.

After hearing her concerns, the therapist simply asked, "If God created you with a brain that can imagine certain thoughts and fuel your own sexual energy and your marriage bed as a result, isn't that a *blessing* rather than a *burden*?"

This woman proclaimed, "I decided I'd rather give up the guilt than give up my marriage, and I'm so glad I did!" The woman continued, "Our sex life over the past twenty years has been amazing, and I have more intense orgasms at seventy-two years old than I've had my whole life!"

I remember thinking, *Yes! Perhaps the best is still yet to come!*

Seriously, I was *so* grateful for her brave confession and cherished words of wisdom! They've stuck with me, and hopefully they'll stick with you too.

Illicit Thoughts

However, we have to be incredibly careful when our erotic sexual fantasies turn into *illicit* fantasies—those involving unlawful or inappropriate relationships, which for Christians means anyone we are not married to.

This definition of illicit fantasy can be disconcerting because a *lot* of people's sexual thoughts often fall into this category. In his book *Who's Been Sleeping in Your Head? The Secret World of Sexual Fantasies*, Brett Kahr reports the results of his large-scale study of the sexual fantasies of 23,000 adults:

- About 90 percent of adults fantasize about someone other than the person with whom they are having sex.
- 41 percent imagine sex with someone else's partner.
- 39 percent fantasize about sex with a work colleague.
- 25 percent fantasize about celebrities.[12]

Gulp. Ninety percent are fantasizing about someone they shouldn't? So can't we just declare that fantasizing about someone other than the person you're having sex with is perfectly normal?

No, we can't. As Christians, our standards of "normal" are measured against the loving guidance of God's Word, not the life most of the world is living, not even inside their heads.

The fact that the vast majority of us are sexually fantasizing about someone we shouldn't have a sexual relationship with at all is a pretty clear indicator that (a) there are a lot of walking wounded who are trying to medicate their emotional pain through sexual fantasy and that (b) this book is long overdue.

These three categories for classifying our fantasies—autoerotic, erotic, and illicit—should provide some clear framework for sifting through our sexual thoughts and determining if any mental editing is in order. The following quiz will provide some practice and will help you solidify this grid in your mind.

Drawing Boundary Lines

Here are ten sample fantasies. Draw appropriate boundary lines around these activities by classifying them as either:

(a) Autoerotic: a random sexual thought that occurs naturally without external stimulation; can be easily managed and should not be cause for guilt
(b) Erotic: a fantasy intended to arouse yourself or your marriage partner; no need for guilt as long as activity is approved of by both spouses
(c) Illicit: a sexual fantasy that would not be approved of by your spouse or by God because of the context of the relationship

____ 1. A teenager who experiences graphic wet dreams while going through puberty

____ 2. A wife who imagines that it might be enjoyable to try a new sexual position with her husband

____ 3. A man who has a sexual dream about his secretary, but would never act on it

____ 4. A female college student who masturbates to thoughts of having sex with her college professor

____ 5. A couple who decides to use pornographic images of others to heat things up in the bedroom

____ 6. A couple who decides to role-play certain characters together to add some variety to the sexual repertoire

____ 7. A man who voyeuristically watches women enter and exit a public restroom, storing those visual images for future masturbation fantasies

____ 8. A woman who goes online to find men who are eager to stroke her ego with some spicy cyber-conversation

____ 9. A husband and wife getting away on vacation so they can indulge in all the sex they want without children in the house

____ 10. A husband and wife who invite another couple to go on vacation together, hoping it could lead to swapping partners

Answers:

1. A
2. B
3. A
4. C
5. C
6. B
7. C
8. C
9. B
10. C

A SENSE OF REAL SAFETY

Granted, psychology tells us that all sexual fantasy is "safe," and by that I simply mean there is no risk for sexually transmitted infections, no chance of unplanned pregnancy, and no awkward "Will he/she still respect me in the morning?" insecurities.

However, an understanding of how God intends for husbands and wives to relate to one another sexually tells us that sexual fantasy can be *too* safe. When we rely on fantasy rather than putting forth the effort to connect with another human being, we can easily forget how to risk, how to be real, how to be vulnerable, and how to love. We can too easily withdraw into ourselves, creating a relational vacuum that only leaves us lonely, isolated, and ultimately depressed. Therefore, drawing boundary lines between appropriate and inappropriate fantasies is vital to the health and vitality of our relationships.

Perhaps you are wondering, *What if some of my own fantasies fall into unsafe or inappropriate categories? What then?* Don't panic. The goal of this book isn't to judge you, keep score of your mental activities, or even call out-of-bounds on you. The goal is to help you dive deeper into the rich symbolism behind your fantasies so that you will be better equipped to face them and win rather than feel defeated by them.

So read on, as we further explore the various faces behind even our most illicit sexual fantasies.

BEHIND THE CURTAIN: RETRAINING OUR BRAINS

When sexual fantasies feel more like a burden than a blessing, the momentary pleasure they provide can pale in comparison to the long-term anxiety they create. But with focused effort, our brains can be retrained to go in alternative (yet still pleasurable) directions.

Remember, a fantasy is simply a story in our heads, and *we* are the narrators of those stories. We decide how the stories take shape, what characters are involved, how we respond to them, and how long the scene goes on before it's served its purpose and the curtain comes down. We are in complete control.

We can always distract our brains away from invasive fantasies as we are going about our day. Men especially have to become masters at this since sexual thoughts occur far more frequently in the male brain.

But what about when you are actually *having* sex . . . and *sex* is exactly what you want to think about? Can you edit or even silence unwanted fantasies altogether? Indeed, you have that power by simply . . .

- *taking your time.* You often resort to fantasy when you feel the need to rush the process and race to the finish line. Time restraints create stress, and the brain often turns to fantasy simply as a way to cope with that stress. Eliminate the lack-of-time stress altogether, and you may eliminate the need for fantasy altogether as well.
- *opening your eyes.* If you are troubled by how your mind is drifting away from your spouse into someone else's direction, open your eyes, turn on a dim light, and bring your brain back to reality. This is your beloved, your marriage bed, your time to delight and be delighted in the presence of your partner. Choose to bask in this reality rather than in an unwanted fantasy.
- *engaging your sense of hearing.* Music is an incredibly sensual tool, especially for women who are typically more

stimulated by what they *hear* than by what they *see*. By playing music that you find intimately relaxing or even energizing, your brain entertains the lyrics and the melody rather than an extraneous fantasy. If you find music too distracting to focus on your partner, simply allow yourself to make noises while making love. The vocal sounds of a sexually charged couple thoroughly enjoying one another can be all the arousal you need!

- *changing positions.* Your brain can begin to wander when you get too comfortable in bed, just as it can in class when you get too comfortable at your desk. By moving your body around and increasing blood flow, you stimulate the brain to remain focused on the subject at hand.
- *focusing on your breathing.* The brain can be stimulated to concentrate on what you're doing by simply taking a few deep breaths, focusing on your inhalation and exhalation. Just as deep breathing helps you remain mentally present, focused, and sharp during physical exercise or while driving a car, the same is true in the bedroom.
- *interrupting the reward cycle.* If you no longer want to orgasm to thoughts that ultimately bring guilt and shame, then don't. No one is holding a gun to your head until you climax. Explain to your spouse that you may decide to disengage momentarily from the sexual experience for a hot shower or a cup of tea or some other relaxing ritual. Don't encourage the brain to entertain certain fantasies by rewarding it with an orgasmic response. Once you are feeling more in control of what thoughts are in your mind, return to your lovemaking. This could take some practice, but it is an effective way to teach your brain what *you* want it to find pleasurable, not vice versa.[13]

If you enjoy a certain fantasy but are bothered by a specific element of it, try altering the story just a few degrees to bring it in line with your moral values or comfort zone. For example, you can alter an entire story line:

- *Change the dynamic.* Perhaps you want to make sure that no one is being forced or hurt in your fantasy. Instead of being victimized by an attacker or abuser, change the fantasy to merely a role-play where you are *pretending* to be victimized but know that you are really in complete control of all that is taking place. Instead of raping or seducing someone in your fantasy, tweak it such that a prior agreement took place and now the person is only *playing* hard to get, but you know beyond a doubt that he or she has every intention of a mutually consenting sexual encounter with you.
- *Change the age of characters.* If the fantasy involves you as a child or teen character with an older adult (as is often the case with sexual abuse victims), make the adult a few years younger and yourself a few years older each time the fantasy comes to mind, until the ages are close enough that the sexual experience would no longer be considered sexually abusive in any way.[14]
- *Change the identity of characters.* Just as the star of any show has an understudy, you can always substitute your spouse as the main star in your fantasies. The sexy college professor can turn out to be your husband after all. (Who knew he looked so good in a salt-and-pepper beard and horn-rimmed glasses?) Or your wife can play the mental role of the hot babe in the hotel lobby who can't take her eyes off you. (We'll talk more about roles and archetypes in the next chapter.)

Consider these suggestions as mental disciplines to help you strengthen your sexual character. And just like any other strength-building exercise, they'll require practice and perseverance. It may mean that you don't reach climax nearly as quickly as before when fantasies raced through your brain unfiltered and unedited. But the enormous pride and pleasure you will experience by fully integrating your thought life, sex life, and spiritual life will be well worth every ounce of mental energy invested.

3

The Faces Behind Sexual Fantasies

At least a couple of times each week, I go on a four-mile bike ride along a nearby community trail. I pass dozens of people along the way, always announcing, "Passing on your left," as a courtesy and to avoid a collision.

Occasionally I'll approach someone walking along and think, *Hey, do I know that person?* But I simply can't tell from the back. So as I pass by on my bicycle, I glance sideways to see the person's face. Only then will I recognize him or her as a familiar friend or complete stranger.

Looking into people's faces is the only way to identify them, and the same is true with our fantasies. However, there are several faces to consider, not just the object of our intimate thought. There are five faces we need to examine if we are to fully understand the multiple layers of our fantasies: Satan, the object, the archetype, the self, and God.

"THE DEVIL MADE ME DO IT!"

While it's easy to assume that all of our sexual fantasies are simply Satan's way of attacking us, let's be real. Sometimes Satan doesn't need any help. We are perfectly capable of falling prey to inappropriate fantasies on our own. Jesus said that evil thoughts come not from *outside* ourselves but from *within our own hearts* (Mark 7:21). But it is so much easier to pass the buck and blame Satan, isn't it? That way we don't have to take responsibility for our own thoughts and actions.

Although Satan is definitely responsible for many sexual distortions, which we will discuss in a moment, let's not be paranoid enough to think that there is a devil waiting for us behind every bush. I have learned that Satan and his band of demons are limited in size and strength. Their population has not grown because demons are not physically capable of reproducing themselves.

Satan and his demons are not omnipresent or omniscient like God is. In other words, they can't be everywhere at all times, and although they may be able to see our actions, they can't read our minds or know our innermost thoughts. We can rest secure in the truth of 1 John 4:4, that "He who is in you [God] is greater than he who is in the world [Satan]" (NKJV).

However, we can't make the mistake of completely underestimating Satan's power. Let's recall how quickly he made his move to mess things up for us and how our sexuality was his prime target.

In Genesis 2:24–25, we see how God gave Adam and Eve the perfectly sublime gift of their sexuality, and He gave them free rein to fully enjoy one another's bodies without guilt, shame, or inhibition:

> So a man will leave his father and mother and be united with his wife, and the two will become one body.
>
> The man and his wife were naked, but they were not ashamed. (NCV)

God's first step toward fulfilling His divine, overall plan was forming the heavens and the earth, providing a place for mankind to dwell. His second step was the actual creation of man and woman, marriage, and sex. This pattern and plan would produce what God longed for most—people to whom He could reveal Himself and with whom He could be in relationship.

But it didn't take long for Satan to try to build a very different kind of relationship with these same people. In the very next chapter we see Satan slither into the Garden of Eden with a crafty plan to confuse Eve first, then Adam, about God's expectation that they should *not* eat from the tree of knowledge (Gen. 3:1–6).

Scripture tells us that once Adam and Eve disobeyed God, their eyes were opened to their own nakedness, and they were filled with such shame that they felt the need to cover themselves and hide from God (Gen. 3:7–10). This was the first fallacy that Satan introduced into the human mind—that our bodies and our sexuality are something we should be ashamed of.

But he didn't stop there. As the book of Genesis continues to unfold, we see Satan distorting sexuality all the more through the introduction of seven further fallacies:

- polygamy (Gen. 4:19)
- homosexuality (Gen. 19:5)
- fornication (Gen. 38:16–18)
- rape (Gen. 34:2)
- prostitution (Gen. 38:15)

- incest (Gen. 19:30–32)
- evil seduction (Gen. 39:7)

Having more than one marriage partner, engaging in sex with someone of the same gender, indulging in sex outside of marriage, having sex as an act of force, using sex as an act of bartering, being intimate with someone young enough to be your child or old enough to be your parent, using sex appeal to lure someone into a forbidden act—aren't these the very things that most illicit sexual fantasies are made of? It's time that we woke up to the fact that we play right into Satan's schemes when we accept these types of fantasies as normal or simply as fodder for more intense orgasms.

Some of our sexual fantasies fall directly in line with this distorted thinking simply because we are fallen sons and daughters of Adam and Eve. However, understanding the deeper meaning behind *why* these activities would appeal to someone in the first place can be incredibly insightful—perhaps, even freeing, believe it or not. If that's hard for you to imagine, the next several chapters may hold a boatload of surprises for you.

But for now, let's move on to consider other, more obvious, faces.

THE FACES IN OUR FANTASIES

People commonly assume that when we experience a dream, fantasy, or random thought, the mental experience is really all about the persons whose faces we saw or about our relationships with them.

Who are these people invading our fantasies? That can change from day to day or even hour to hour. As we mentioned in the previous chapter, these faces are most often people other than our spouses—usually someone else's partner, a neighbor, a friend, a coworker, a celebrity, or perhaps no one we recognize at all but more of a mysterious figure or composite image.

At first glance into our fantasy world, if we recognize the face we may panic and wonder, *Why would I dream/fantasize about that person? What does this mean?* But more than a first glance is needed. We fantasize as a way to fulfill unconscious psychological needs, so the actual identifiable face isn't nearly as important as the role that face is playing in our mental scenario.

A better question to ask would be, "What role does this person play in my fantasy? What is this person doing, and why would my brain venture in that direction?"

WHY ARE YOU HERE?

Psychologists call these imagined roles *archetypes*, which are defined in Jungian psychology as "a collectively inherited unconscious idea, pattern of thought, image, etc., universally present in individual psyches."[1]

In the book *Inner Work: Using Dreams and Active Imagination for Personal Growth*, Robert Johnson gives further insight into archetypes and the roles they play in an individual's mind. There is often a war within among various characters, like the child or the mother, the knight and the fair maiden, or the monk and the drunk, and so on.

> We might say that these represent human possibilities, aspects of human characteristics that are common to all.
>
> Here we encounter the *archetypes*: the universal patterns or tendencies in the human unconscious that find their way into our individual psyches and form us. They are actually the psychological building blocks of energy that combine together to create the individual psyche. Here are the type of the child, the

> type of the mother, the universal virgin, and the universal tart, all flowing through the personality of one individual.
>
> In our dreams [and fantasies], they join the archetypal hero or heroine, the priest, the scoundrel. Each of them adds a different richness to our character and has a different truth to tell. Each represents our own, individual version of the universal forces that combine to create a human life.[2]

Another way to understand archetypes is simply to imagine the faces in our fantasies as nothing more than projection screens. The roles that we assign these faces/screens come from our own collection of mental movies. So the fantasy isn't about that particular person. It's about what that person represents in your mind or how you recognize certain characteristics about that person that are either present (or absent) inside of you.

It's these projection screens and mental movies that provide the richest material for coaching sessions. Many clients come to me *after* they've crossed a line, having acted out sexually with the object of their fantasy. They gave this other person way too much power and focused on the projection screen instead of the movie that was playing in their own heads at the time. Whenever you pursue another person as the solution to your fantasy problem, you're only complicating the problem, adding more layers of emotional baggage to sift through.

Think of the nature of a projection screen. It's an inanimate object. It can't hurt you. It just hangs on the wall and lets you project whatever you want onto it. The screen has no preference or will of its own, so it doesn't pose any threat or harm. If we recognize it for what it is—just a screen, and that's all—we won't feel the need to panic when our mental movies begin playing on it. Instead, we can focus on the movie, not the screen.

If we all treated our fantasies in such a way by taking the shock and sting out of them and recognizing the real dynamic at hand, we wouldn't feel the need to act out inappropriately with the person we are fantasizing about. We would simply focus on the movie we are playing, not the object, screen, or face the movie is playing on.

Put another way, consider your reaction if you walked into a room and caught a teenager projecting a pornographic movie onto a screen. You wouldn't get mad at or blame the screen, would you? No, you would take issue with the movie being projected and, more specifically, with the one who chose the movie, correct?

When it comes to our fantasies, *we* are the ones who choose the movie. The screen simply allows us to recognize what movie is playing. This process provides clues to the plots we are trying to project onto others, clues to the personal "soul work" that the unconscious is inviting us into.

So will you pay attention and watch and listen to your life's movies? Will you accept the invitation to expose the deeper meaning behind your sexual thoughts and let them heal you, rather than hurt you?"

I faced these very questions over a decade ago. I was thrown for a loop by my own scary thoughts as I began involuntarily fantasizing about a particular man who lived nearby. I'll call him Zach. This man would frequently knock on the door and ask to hunt wild game on our land. But before heading to the woods with his rifle, he'd bend over backward to engage me in lengthy conversations.

I confess, I initially soaked up the attention like a dry sponge. It felt good to have someone wanting to talk to me. It eased some of my loneliness. But it also stole too many of my brain cells and began gnawing away at my soft conscience.

Rocking in the porch swing with my husband one evening, I tearfully confessed that I had been having emotionally charged thoughts about Zach, and I asked that he make me responsible never to act on them.

Greg responded, "Shannon, you're the one studying counseling and Imago therapy, which teaches that certain people fit a 'mental mold' based on your childhood relationships. Don't you get it? Zach fits your mental mold. He looks just like your brother, and he acts just like your dad. This isn't about Zach at all. It's about you and your relationships with these important men in your life. Fix those, and you'll fix the fantasy issue."

I was stunned by how Greg had hit the nail on the head. Zach was merely my projection screen. I didn't need to fear the screen (although he may have been projecting a few of his own mental movies onto my screen as well, so caution wasn't a bad idea). I needed to pay attention to the movie I was projecting onto him.

After prayerful consideration I recognized the plot of my movie. Attention and conversation were things I had always longed for more of from my dad and brother as I was growing up. But letting Zach try to fill that hole instead of going to the source not only was a dangerous proposition but also, ultimately, would have been a fruitless endeavor. It most likely would have led to some sort of emotional or sexual affair, which would have made me feel horrible about myself and driven an even bigger wedge between me and the men in my life—not just my dad and brother but also my husband. No, I hadn't lost my keys to fulfillment under Zach's streetlight. I'd lost those in my family of origin, and that was the only logical place to search.

So instead of letting myself get caught up in conversations with Zach, I consistently kept things short, sweet, and to the point, then would walk back into the house, leaving him standing there in the yard with hunting rifle in hand, if necessary. I also began inviting my extended family over for social gatherings more often so that we could begin making more memories together and building stronger relationships.

So in a way I have to be grateful for that fantasy. It was an incredible learning experience about what my soul was really craving. It revealed to me a felt need in my life, fortunately, while there was still an opportunity to heal this hurt. Many folks never come to this realization until *after* their loved one is no longer alive to build a better relationship.

In addition to recognizing those other faces in our fantasies as mere projection screens, let's look a little more closely at the common denominator among most all of our sexual thoughts—ourselves.

THE MAN (OR WOMAN) IN THE MIRROR

As previously mentioned, blaming Satan for inappropriate thoughts would be so much easier than what I am about to suggest, but if we are really going to expose the deeper meaning behind our sexual fantasies, some soul work is required.

In order to consider the roots of our thinking, we must allow ourselves to descend into the dark places, the hard places, that we (ourselves and the church) have tried diligently to avoid in the past. We must learn to live in the tension that our fantasies often create. We must identify not just the surface of the fantasy but the very *source* of the inner tension—in other words, why we feel the way we do about the thoughts that we have. That can be found only as we descend into some of the soul's unexplored chasms.

In *A Little Book on the Human Shadow*, Robert Bly says that when we are born, we receive a long bag we drag behind us.[3] We spend the first half of our lives filling this long bag full of our personal paradigms and secrets. We spend the last half of our lives removing those very things, one at a time, holding them up to the light, examining them, and trying to make sense out of them. In doing so we are sometimes able to unlearn the fallacies we have adopted along the way, becoming healthier, safer people in the process.

One of the things I believe we often put in that long bag is the notion that we are either "all good" or "all bad"—one extreme or the other. It doesn't take much to realize that we can't be all good, all the time, so we deduce that we must be all bad. This idea that we must exist on one end of the spectrum or the other is yet another example of extreme thinking. Such a dichotomy hearkens back to what I explained through the lion dream in the introduction to this book; we can't be too liberal or too legalistic. We must find a healthy balance in the middle of these two extremes.

The way to remedy this dichotomous thinking is to accept the fact that we aren't one or the other. We are *both*. We all possess an internal "bright light" because we are made in the image of God, but we also possess an internal "shadow self" because of the fall of man. We are a combination of good and bad, light and dark, hope and hopelessness. Our fantasies certainly reflect that, don't they?

Ignoring this shadow self is going to have the same effect as ignoring a child who's desperate for attention. It's only going to get all the more unruly until it is recognized. I believe that ignoring this shadow self to the point that it *demands* attention is exactly what has caused many Christian leaders (and followers) to stumble and fall headlong into sordid affairs and humiliating sex scandals. What if leaders such as Bill Clinton, Jim Bakker, Jimmy Swaggart, and Ted Haggard had paused long enough not just to *ask* but also to *answer* the questions, "Why am I tempted to act out sexually with this person? What mental movie am I trying to project onto her?"

Sometimes the smartest thing to do is stop ignoring your shadow self, turn and face it, acknowledge its presence, and say,

Okay, I see you. You don't have to keep pestering me. You have my attention. What is it that you want exactly? What are you here to teach me? How can I help you?

Whatever feelings arise, greet them, regardless of how scary or painful. Pick each emotion up like a crying child. Hold it. Attend to it. Comfort it. Befriend your shadow self rather than reject it. With this level of personal honesty, you may be able to bring into consciousness what your unconscious has been trying to say to you all along through your thoughts and dreams.

In the book *Inner Work*, Robert Johnson explains the reasoning behind the relationship most of us have with this shadow self:

> How the shadow appears in a dream [or fantasy] depends on the ego's attitude. For example, if a man's attitude is friendly toward his inner shadow, and he is willing to grow and change, his shadow will often appear as a helpful friend, a "buddy," a tribal brother who helps him in his adventures, backs him up, and teaches him skills. If he is trying to repress the shadow, it will usually appear as a hateful enemy, a brute or monster who attacks him in his dreams. The same principles apply to a woman. Depending on her relationship to her shadow, she may appear as a loving sister or as a frightful witch.[4]

I do believe it is possible to befriend the shadow self and bring healing into these unexplored gorges of our souls by being mindful of them, by giving them time and space to tell us why they even exist. I don't believe God created humans so that we could stick our heads in the sand when we saw something in ourselves that seems scary or shame inducing. After all, there's nowhere we can run, nowhere we can hide, to get away from ourselves or our sexuality. But perhaps we can learn to boldly face our unexplored depths, observe our sexual thoughts and fantasies, and assign them accurate meaning without getting caught up in them or swept away by them.

With the Holy Spirit's guidance we can hold these recurring mental images outside of ourselves, objectify them, and analyze them with the wisdom of not just a researcher but the inventor. Yes, we have invented these figments of our own imaginations, and we hold the key to unlocking their mysteries.

As the author of this book, I authorize you to explore these chasms. No one else can do it but you, not even the best counselor or spiritual leader. No one else can connect the dots that need to be connected in order to recognize the big picture. No one else can accurately narrate the story that is uniquely yours.

THE FACE THAT DRAWS US

The final face we need to explore is obviously the most important—that of God. As bizarre as it may sound, I believe that if we peel back every layer of every fantasy, what we will discover at the core of our sexual longings is a much deeper spiritual longing.

What we ultimately crave isn't an intimate encounter with flesh and blood that will eventually age and rot. That's a poor substitute. What we ultimately crave is an intimate encounter with the eternal life-giving spirit of God. We will never be satisfied settling for less.

> The pursuit of purity is not about the suppression of lust, but about the reorientation of one's life to a larger goal.
> *—Dietrich Bonhoeffer*

Yet sometimes we do. We settle for what this world has to offer us in the here and now because we lose our vision of what the next world will be like—our perfect heavenly home, where unresolved pain will no longer exist and the gravitational pull of sin and separation from God will no longer have any effect on us.

And when we do settle, what is God's attitude toward us? As He witnesses the plethora of provocative images that prance through our brains, trying to medicate the pain of being a fallen creature living in a fallen world, does His face possess a look of shock? Horror? Disdain? Disgust?

Absolutely not. To get a crystal-clear picture of God's face as we wrestle with our sexual thoughts and temptations, we need only look to Hebrews 4:14–16:

> Since we have a great high priest, Jesus the Son of God, who has gone into heaven, let us hold on to the faith we have. For our high priest is able to understand our weaknesses. He was tempted in every way that we are, but he did not sin. Let us, then, feel very sure that we can come before God's throne where there is grace. There we can receive mercy and grace to help us when we need it. (NCV)

Did you catch that? Jesus has walked this earth, wrapped in the same hormonally charged flesh as God has wrapped us in. He's been here, experienced that gravitational pull. He understands. He sympathizes. He welcomes us into His presence. He offers mercy, grace, and unconditional love. The look on His face is that of sheer *compassion*.

Seeking the Face of God Through the Body of Christ

People with sexual struggles often find it difficult to connect on an intimate spiritual level with others, but this is precisely the best prescription for understanding and overcoming any issue. Our sexual wounds originate *in relationship*, so we're more likely to find healing *in relationship*.

But it's easy to look out into the sea of faces filling the pews and assume, *These people have really got their act together!* That sweet family with six homeschooled children and a minivan, no way have they ever had to deal with any sexually inappropriate thoughts or behaviors in their holy household. That immaculately groomed guy in the finely tailored suit and shiny shoes, surely his money has insulated him from sexual dysfunction. That woman in the green polka dot dress and string of pearls, surely her husband is the only man she ever thinks about kissing her ruby red lips.

It's easy for most people to step into any church and think, *There's no one here who struggles with sexual thoughts, feelings, and fantasies like I do. Not a single person who could possibly understand, so why bother coming here? So I can hide behind a mask and wallow privately in my personal guilt? No, thank you. I can do that at home alone.*

If this is your thinking about church, I would like to confidently assure you that your impression is, quite frankly, dead wrong. Those homeschooling families often have sexual skeletons in their closets dating back multiple generations. Many of those well-dressed businessmen are dragged into my coaching office by their wives to peel back the layers of their pornography addictions. And those ladies with ruby red lips are often confessing to me that they're wrestling with sexual thoughts and fantasies that would absolutely make your toes curl. They are really no different than any other sexual being on the planet.

We all have our struggles. We all have our secrets. We are far more alike than we are different.

I would love to wave a magic wand and completely influence church culture all over the world, making the church widely known as the Go-To Place for sexual healing and wholeness. But I am not that influential. I am one writer, with one voice.

I am ambitious enough to believe that if I can influence just one spiritual leader to open the lines of communication about all-things-sexual with his or her congregation . . . or one follower of Christ to open lines of communication with a spouse or child or friend or fellow believer, then we can truly change the world one marriage, one family, one church and one community at a time.

God recently gave me a crystal-clear glimpse into that face of compassion while I was speaking at a women's retreat. As ladies from all walks of life worshipped together, the lyrics of a particular song struck a slight chord of regret in my heart. As we sang about longing to sit at the feet of Jesus and share intimate moments with Him, guilt from my past reared its ugly head as if it still had a place in my life. (It doesn't since Jesus removed that guilt on the cross long ago, but it still likes to pretend on occasion.)

I whispered to God, "I'm so sorry for the way I've run to other men in the past, seeking to share intimate moments with *them* for satisfaction rather than running to *You*, Lord!"

A mental vision came to me of a lost little girl in a grocery store, searching for the security of her mom or dad, mistaking a stranger's leg for that of her parent's, wrapping her arms around tightly, then looking up and realizing her error in judgment, feeling mortified, scared, and more lost than ever, and then recognizing her real parent down the aisle and running at breakneck speed into welcoming arms.

I sensed God asking, *Remember when your daughter made that very mistake?* Indeed, I remembered it happening with both of my children on more than one occasion. *And what did you feel toward your child in that moment, Shannon? Anger? Betrayal? Disgust?* God asked. *Of course not. Neither do I feel angry or betrayed or disgusted by your mistakes. You delight Me greatly by recognizing and running to Me now, and that's all that matters to Me,* our heavenly Father lovingly explained.

We often fantasize about and run toward many other sources for the comfort and solace that only God can give. And we *still* end up lost and longing for more than is possible on this side of heaven. But isn't it wonderful to know that regardless of what we have wrapped our arms around in the past, God presently and will forevermore welcome us with open arms? He alone can fully satisfy the desperate desires of the human heart. Even mine. And yes, even yours.

BEHIND THE CURTAIN: SOPHIA'S LAYERS OF LONELINESS

While Sophia was dating Simon, she absolutely idolized him. Visions of white wedding dresses and white picket fences danced in her lovesick head night and day. She couldn't wait to become his wife, just like in the Disney fairy tales she had been mesmerized by as a child.

But as she fantasized about what married life would be like, she never dreamed of several bitter realities that eventually surfaced, such as the fact that when Simon came home stressed over work, which was often, he'd seek refuge in either his video game system or the television.

Many weeks he would waste fifteen to twenty hours engaged in these mental escapes, leaving Sophia feeling incredibly lonely and rejected. Because she had been taught to "submit to your husband" by her Christian parents, she didn't feel as if she had the right to demand a better relationship. As her feelings of isolation and desperation grew deeper, Sophia's brain naturally gravitated far beyond her white picket fence. She began fantasizing about some of Simon's friends, who seemed much more mature and emotionally available in comparison. Not only was one in particular more emotionally available, but he also made himself physically available at opportune times.

"I knew in my heart that fooling around with one of my husband's closest friends was a foolish move, but my head justified it in such a wide variety of ways:

- No one has to know.
- Even if Simon finds out, how can he blame me?
- He'd do the same thing if given the chance.
- I deserve to feel loved and desired.
- Perhaps this is my ticket out of this miserable marriage!"

Unfortunately it wasn't Sophia's ticket out of the marriage because the friend was so racked with guilt afterward that he stopped coming around. Another of Simon's friends, completely oblivious to what had previously transpired (or was he?), saw that Sophia was incredibly frustrated in her marriage and assumed correctly that she must be sexually frustrated as well. He pursued, and Sophia loved the attention and made it easy for him, in spite of the fact that she knew how painful such a mistake had proven to be last time. History repeated itself, and this friend eventually stopped coming around as well. That's when Sophia drew another close friend into her emotional void.

"After the third affair, I knew there would be no salvaging our marriage. 'Cheat on me once, shame on you; cheat on me twice, shame on me; cheat on me a third time, it's divorce time.' I was so filled with bitterness and animosity toward Simon for all that he'd done—or *not* done!—but he also had every right to feel the same way toward me for all that I'd done," Sophia tearfully conceded.

Although Simon certainly played a large part in causing Sophia to feel so lonely in their marriage, I challenged Sophia to consider why the fantasy of being with another man felt so overwhelming that she'd actually *act* on it—three times—which had done far more damage than good to her self-esteem. I wondered if she recognized how she had used her sex appeal and her body to barter for the attention and affection she craved.

"The fantasy was never as much about having sex with these guys, although it occasionally drifted in that direction, as it was about them simply wanting to be with me, to talk to me, to get to know me and find me interesting . . . no, to find me absolutely *irresistible*," Sophia realized.

"Wasn't this something you could have expected more of from your husband?" I asked.

"Yes, but I didn't know how to fight for it. I didn't even know how to *ask* for it. I assumed he should just know. But when he didn't catch on, I chose to pout and act all passive-aggressive. It didn't work. It just enabled him to keep his head in the TV or computer screen," Sophia explained.

Although the temptation is always to figure out what the *other* person did wrong and why, it's usually a much better use of time and energy to figure out why *we* act the way we do in relationships and why we fantasize in certain directions. Sometimes the only way to peel back the layers of disillusionment and disappointment is to completely get away from all distractions. Then we can more readily discover this core driving factor behind our fantasies and temptations, and we can mentally tap into our innermost thoughts and feelings about ourselves, and most especially about ourselves in relationship with other people.

I suggested Sophia take a four-day sabbatical to spend time alone with God, her own thoughts, and the hurting little girl trapped inside her adult body so she could discover her core driving factor. After completing my sentence, I literally heard her gasp for air over the phone; then there was dead silence for several seconds.

"Sophia, what are you thinking and feeling right now?" I inquired.

It took her a few moments, and then she responded, "Panic."

"Why are you panicked? What is it about this exercise that scares you?" I asked.

Taking plenty of time to sift through her thoughts, she eventually spoke up. "I'm having a hard time breathing right now. The idea of being completely alone scares me."

"Why, Sophia? Did something happen at some point in your life when you were left alone?"

"No. It's just that I've never been alone, at least not successfully," she responded.

"Tell me what you mean by 'not successfully,'" I coaxed.

"I was a middle child, so there was always an older or younger sibling around. My mother didn't work outside the home, so she was always around too. Whenever I got punished, my mom would send me to my room to be alone, but I'd pitch such a fit that she'd cave in and at least leave the door open and turn some music on to soothe me. I was a very well-behaved child simply because the idea of being sent to my room alone was petrifying to me."

"And how old were you when you married Simon?"

"We were pretty young, but I thought I was totally ready for marriage. I think that, maybe, I married Simon so early in life partly because I couldn't stand the thought of ever living by myself, not even in a college dorm room," she deduced.

"And when Simon's attentions were completely consumed by something other than you, did you feel alone even though he was in the living room?"

"That's exactly how I felt, but I didn't put two and two together that his emotional disconnection was making me feel as panicked as if I was physically by myself."

"Did Simon have to travel often with work?"

"No, very rarely. But the one time he was gone overnight was when the first affair happened. I didn't realize that my eagerness to let this friend into our house while Simon was away was more about alleviating my panic over being alone than about having sex with someone else. I don't think that's what I really wanted, but it was obviously what he wanted, so I went along to keep him around as long as possible."

"So when the first friend disappeared, how did you handle that loss and the return of your loneliness?" I asked.

"Rather than sit around and stew over it while Simon watched television, I chose to go out with my girlfriends. This is how the second affair got started, when I ran into another of Simon's friends while out that night. It really wasn't about sex with him, either. I just wanted to keep him interested in getting to know me . . . in hanging around. Boy, did that backfire," she acknowledged. "Now Simon is incredibly lonely, too, because I've scared his two best friends off by having affairs with them. I feel horrible."

I asked Sophia if she thought history might continue to repeat itself if she didn't get a grip on her overwhelming fear of being alone. She recognized the pattern and could easily predict that the future would be more of the same if something didn't change in the present. "I guess I can never rely on any husband to be 100 percent physically and emotionally available to me twenty-four/seven, huh?" she realized.

The sabbatical was incredibly difficult, but Sophia managed to spend four days alone with nothing but her Bible, her journal, and her innermost thoughts and feelings. No television, telephone, Internet, or iPod. Just she and God.

"I survived!" Sophia boasted, proud of conquering a fear that had haunted her for more than twenty years. "The first couple of days I felt like I'd come out of my skin, but as I settled in with my Bible and journal, I began recognizing how God was *always* with His people, constantly watching out for them, giving them victory in battle, miraculously providing for their needs, and pursuing them with His extravagant mercy and unconditional love. I asked God if He has me that squarely in His sights as well, and by the third and fourth days, I could *feel* His presence enveloping me like a soft, handmade patchwork quilt."

I asked Sophia how she felt about being by herself now. She replied, "I don't like it, but I know I'll live through it and will hopefully grow up a lot more as a result. Until I'm okay with being alone, I'm really not okay being in a relationship with anyone else. I can't expect anyone to *know me* until I know myself, and I'm going to continue looking to God for that since He's the One who made me in the first place."

4

Pornography: The Fantasy Factory

It was 5:00 a.m., and I simply could not sleep. The urge was so overwhelming that I knew it would be fruitless to try to return to my slumber. So I gave in.

I tiptoed gingerly from the master bedroom, down the hall, and into the sitting room where I'd have more privacy, attempting the whole way not to let the wood floors creak for fear of waking my husband or son. They didn't need to know what I was doing.

I opened my laptop, pressed the blue-lit button, went online to do a Google search, and found the exact movie I was looking for. I'd eagerly anticipated watching it for weeks, and now, in the quiet morning hours, I would indulge in solitude. I sat there mesmerized for the first twelve minutes, fascinated by the graphic images on the screen. I hadn't seen or heard anything like it before. It was a feast for my senses.

But then I was startled by the sound of footsteps turning the corner from the kitchen, and there in the doorway stood all six feet and seven inches of my husband, hands on his hips and bewildered as to what in the world I'd be watching at five o'clock in the morning. He eased into the room, slid into the chair next to mine, and gently rotated my laptop screen in his direction to satisfy his curiosity. A sheepish smile and shrugged shoulders were all I could muster in response.

Seconds later, once Greg realized what I was watching, a broad grin spread across his face, he rolled his eyes and moaned, "Oh, good grief! You are such a geek, Shannon! You're the only person I know who'd get up in the wee hours of the morning to watch a *NOVA* special on PBS about interpreting dreams!"

I confess, I *am* a bit of a geek in that regard. The topic of dreams and fantasies has put me on a relentless pursuit of any helpful information I can find.

Unfortunately, fantasies have also put many others on some relentless pursuits, sometimes in the dark hours of the night, but obviously for very different reasons. My friend Elle Emerson (her alias) rolled over in her bed one cold December night to discover her husband gone. Hearing the sound of the TV, she tiptoed down the stairs and peeked around the corner. She explains, "The images I saw on the screen sent chills up my spine—images incredibly crude and graphic. Porn, welcomed into our home for a nightcap, had unlocked the door to my husband's heart and was devouring his soul. Sinking to my knees, I cried out, 'Please stop this! You're breaking my heart!' Uncontrollable sobs escaped from somewhere deep within as I ran back to our room and begged God to save our marriage."

Elle later wrote the following blog post to encourage couples who are entrenched in a similar fantasy fallacy:

> I cried the first time I watched the movie *A Beautiful Mind*. I couldn't believe how much the life of a man living with schizophrenia and his wife struggling to help him mirrored

the life of a husband struggling with sexual brokenness and his wife trying to love him through it. The similarities, uncanny.

In *A Beautiful Mind*, John's imagination has turned toward the direction of self-destruction. As schizophrenia slowly devours his mind, it also threatens to destroy the love he shares with his wife. Simply stated, John is slowly losing his grip on all that's real and beautiful in his life.

Make no mistake about it, Internet pornography is the crack cocaine of sexual addictions. It enters the body through the eye at lightning speed, packing an endorphin punch so powerful that it knocks a man's sexual libido clear out of the park each and every time he chooses to fix his gaze on sexually charged images. Porn hits a home run with every man, every time, guaranteed. And in the process healthy relationships between husbands and their wives are sometimes destroyed. Men free-fall further than they ever would have wagered. Some men reap the total destruction of everything they held dear in their lives. Death of a ministry. Death of a dream. Death of a marriage. Death of a beautiful mind. Death of all that's real to him.

Men who use porn are hooked on fantasy. And they are hooked on the sexual high they get from using porn for sexual release. But false intimacy and real intimacy were never meant to co-exist peacefully in the same heart. Humans were never created to live with such duplicity.

In the movie, when Alicia realizes that John has lost his grip on reality, she knows that the only way she can help him is to show him the difference between what is real and what is fantasy. Alicia says to John, "Do you know what's real? This." (She strokes *his* face with her hand.) "This." (She strokes *her* face with his hand.) "This." (She puts her hand over his heart.)

> "This is real . . . Maybe the part that knows the waking from the dream . . . maybe it's in here."
>
> Alicia then pleads with John, "I need to believe that something extraordinary is possible."
>
> Do you see it? Alicia knows that a beautiful mind flows out of a heart that lives for *what's real* instead of living for a fantasy.
>
> When a man is hooked on porn and waist deep in the sickening sludge of sexual brokenness, he needs someone extraordinary to awaken his heart again to what's real. When a woman is betrayed and feels like her heart has flatlined, she needs someone extraordinary to pull her through to life again. Jesus is just the man for both of these jobs. He alone can do the extraordinary.[1]

Of course, it isn't always the husband who's hooked on porn. I coach many women who are living in their own porn-torn world, struggling to find the freedom they long for.

The fastest route to freedom is to pull back the veil on what really goes on in the fantasy factory of pornography—both in the performers (the exhibitionists) and in the audience (the voyeurs).

WHAT'S REAL FOR EXHIBITIONISTS

Porn actors often get reeled into making films because of the incredible emotional rush they feel when someone finds them noteworthy or "camera worthy." And not just *one* person but an entire viewing audience. At first glance it's all about getting noticed and being willing to do *anything* to make that happen, regardless of how painful or degrading that *anything* may be.

While I haven't been personally acquainted with a large number of men or women in the porn industry, I've had occasion to speak with a few women through various support group ministries. If one common thread exists among those who've been willing to bare their bodies for the sake of "fulfilling" (and I use that word loosely) other people's fantasies, it's that they've felt incredibly rejected or neglected in the past. Many are teenage runaways or were kicked out of the house by a violent parent, so it's about not just stardom but also survival. Most have been sexually abused already, so the notion of having sex with a stranger in front of a camera for a $1,000 paycheck is preferred to standing in line at a local soup kitchen. One film turns into three or four per month, and prostitution is yet another avenue of fast income for 90 percent of porn stars.[2] Soon they are making more money than they ever thought possible, thus drinking and doing more drugs than ever before—at first for the thrill, but later because they have to numb themselves completely to do what's expected of them on camera.

If you're brave enough to peek inside the real world of porn stars, read *The Empire of Illusion* by Chris Hedges. In a chapter called "The Illusion of Love," Hedges exposes:

- How a forty-five-minute scene requires thirteen hours to tape, so women are exhausted, and their vaginas and anuses are ripped, sore, and bleeding by the time shooting wraps up.[3]
- How female porn stars are paid to fake orgasm because climaxing on the set *never* happens under such humiliating duress.[4]
- How male stars take Viagra or inject a hardening agent into an open vein in the penis to keep it erect for hours at a time, which also becomes necessary at home when having sex with their girlfriends.[5]

- How common it is for women to get pregnant, have abortions, and contract sexually transmitted infections (including HIV), mainly because producers don't want actors wearing condoms. It's too expensive to Photoshop them out of the scenes.[6]

You may wonder, *Why does this matter? I'm not a porn star!* Let's remember that porn actors are people with deeply felt spiritual and emotional needs, just like us. If we as a church could find ways to show them how to *actually heal* the wounds that have driven them toward such exhibitionism, and show them more personally empowering ways to earn a living, imagine how much healthier their personal lives could become, not to mention the lives of their children! (I know it's hard to imagine that porn stars have personal lives and children to raise, but they actually exist on this earth for more reasons than just to fuel illicit fantasies.)

As I contemplate the unthinkable atrocities that humans endure for the sake of fueling the Fantasy Factories—the corporate ones as well as the mental ones in avid consumers' minds—I can't help but feel incredibly grieved over how badly we've been duped. There's simply no bigger fantasy fallacy than the porn industry. Chris Hedges so eloquently explains:

> The porn films are not about sex. . . . There is no acting because none of the women are permitted to have what amounts to a personality. The one emotion they are allowed to display is an unquenchable desire to satisfy men, especially if that desire involves the women's physical and emotional degradation. The lighting in the films is harsh and clinical. Pubic hair is shaved off to give the women the look of younger girls or rubber dolls. Porn, which advertises itself

> as sex, is a bizarre, bleached pantomime of sex. The acts onscreen are beyond human endurance. The scenarios are absurd. The manicured and groomed bodies, the huge artificial breasts, the pouting, oversized lips, the erections that never go down, and the sculpted bodies are unreal. Makeup and production mask blemishes. There are no beads of sweat, no wrinkle lines, no human imperfections. Sex is reduced to a narrow spectrum of sterilized dimensions. It does not include the dank smell of human bodies, the thump of a pulse, taste, breath—or tenderness. Those in the films are puppets, packaged female commodities. . . . Pornography does not promote sex, if one defines sex as a shared act between two partners. It promotes masturbation. It promotes the solitary auto-arousal that precludes intimacy and love. Pornography is about getting yourself off at someone else's expense.[7]

Sorry if this insider's view is shattering your illusions that porn is a great aphrodisiac, but I think it's important that Christians be aware of the bigger picture, especially (a) how we are using and abusing other humans for our own sexual jollies and (b) how it's negatively affecting our ability to experience genuine sexual intimacy in our marriages.

So rather than wasting more time or energy focusing on the *fruit* of sexual fantasies (such as surfing for certain pornographic images), perhaps it's time to consider the *roots*, starting with the deep reasons we are tempted to peek at porn in the first place.

WHAT'S REAL FOR VOYEURS

Why are human beings so fascinated with graphic sexual images? The surface answer is that they make us hot, they turn us on, and they get our motors revving.

But we're not stopping at surface answers in this book. We are diving deeper. Most of us know what sexual images turn us on, but few of us know why. This information is absolutely vital to our spiritual and emotional growth. After all, how can we "take thoughts captive" unless we acknowledge the true nature of those thoughts and seek to fully understand where they come from? How can we break free from their bondage if we ignore the grip they have on us?

Fifty percent of all Christian men and 20 percent of all Christian women are addicted to pornography.[8]

Over the past year I have been interacting with three individuals I would like to tell you about. Although they come from very different backgrounds, they all have one thing in common. Each is addicted to some form of pornography. Although these are not their real names, let me introduce you to them:

- Mitch, a Christian leader in his church and community, who occasionally dons a disguise and drives to a topless bar on the outskirts of town
- Megan, a preteen girl who masturbates several times a week to Internet images of other women masturbating
- Tammy, who uses her company laptop to view porn while traveling, telling herself that this is better than hanging out in the hotel lobby bar and running the risk of an actual affair

Each has asked the same questions: If I'm a Christian, why do I still do this? Why hasn't God given me the strength to stop?

While God *is* perfectly capable of miraculously delivering us from our sexual addictions, this isn't usually how the process works. God invites us to fully participate in this healing work with Him, for our own growth and benefit. A significant amount of soul work on our part is necessary, or else we never will move past the pain of addiction or past the pain that drives us toward porn in the first place. The "Twelve Steps to Recovery" on page 213 will help you begin this process.

> **"Sex begins in the mind and then travels downward."**[9]
> *—Dr. Michael J. Bader*

For now, I suggest that you start by considering these questions:

- What types of images light your fire whether you want them to or not?
- When you feel the need or desire to become sexually aroused, what are a few of the mental images you know you can always rely on to accomplish that goal?
- If you use pornography, what specific scenarios do you surf for?
- Given these scenarios, what are the underlying emotions that you are most likely trying to quell, amplify, or balance with such fantasies?
- Thinking back as far as you can remember, when do you recall feeling these particular emotions before?
- What message could these emotions have been trying to send you?

Here's how these questions have helped our panel of "experts" decipher the exact driving force behind their own pornography addictions.

What's Real for Mitch

Mitch, the Christian leader who occasionally visits a topless bar, says that he never sits up front to gawk at the girls up close.

He prefers to have a lovely lingerie-clad lady approach him in the back of the room, eager to chat with him on a deeply personal level about his thoughts, feelings, and struggles—some sexual, some not. "It's the interest that she shows in me and the safety I feel with her that arouses me sexually," Mitch realizes.

He didn't have to wrestle long when I asked him, "When have you felt so uninteresting to a female audience that you need this fantasy to experience sexual arousal? And how far back does this feeling go?"

> **"Sex is the panacea for most problems in our culture, especially for men. They want to solve every problem, ease every discomfort, and escape every tension with sex. But using sex as a solution never allows us to get to the root of the issue. Instead of repeatedly popping pain-killers to stop headaches, we'd be better off examining *why* we have recurring headaches in the first place."**
> *—Jarratt Major, LMFT*

He said, "The temptation to go to this club is strongest when my wife and I get disconnected, especially if we hit a spot in our relationship when almost every subject is a sensitive one. When she's troubled with me, I simply can't get sexually aroused. I feel like a dud who doesn't know how to make a woman happy, so I go to a bar where I can pay a buck to have someone dispel that myth in my mind."

Mitch went on, "I can recall similar feelings when I was around nine years old. I used to sit on a stool against the wall of our kitchen, rambling on for hours about almost anything with my mother while she was cooking. But I could tell when she'd grow exhausted with my ramblings, and I learned that certain subjects weren't safe to talk about, such as my questions about deep theological issues, my extreme feelings of loneliness, or sex."

By recognizing that his desire to visit the topless bar was actually rooted in his desire to be heard and to feel safe in the presence of a female, Mitch is more motivated to keep lines of communication wide open with his wife. "Taking her out to dinner and making her feel special and safe enough to connect with me may cost me more than a dollar tucked in a dancer's bra once in a while, but it's a worthy investment not to go to bed feeling like a worm that night. Going into the bar was always exhilarating. Walking out and realizing how low I'd stooped for an ego stroke were incredibly deflating."

It feels much safer to look at porn than to look at our own pain, to masturbate than to humbly ask for what we need.

What's Real for Megan

When Megan's mom brought her in for counseling, Megan was riddled with guilt and confusion over why she'd want to "touch her privates" while watching other women do the same. Her Internet searches were never about watching people have sex with each other. Rather, watching a woman bring herself to climax was what fueled Megan's fire. So we figured out that "women taking control of their bodies and their own emotions" was a common theme in Megan's fantasies.

I asked, "Has there been a time when you felt out of control in your life, Megan?" Rolling her eyes, she explained that both she and her mother had felt out of control since she was six. That's when her father was killed in a boating accident, which was painful enough for Megan because she was "daddy's girl." But it was watching her mother wallow in her own grief for the past six years that was more than she could effectively cope with. She wanted to wave a magic wand and erase all her mother's pain, to erase all her own pain, and for both of them to enter into a state of mental bliss where there was no room for death or grief or sadness—the type of mental bliss that pornographic images of women taking control of their bodies and pleasuring themselves could vividly provide. So a click of Megan's mouse became the equivalent to waving that magic wand.

The main problem was that the magic never lasted. The guilt did. So Megan had to learn to ask for what she needed from her mother—a smile, a hug, a shopping trip to the mall where Megan could be the focus, a day without her mother's tears or anger or extreme perfectionism driving Megan into her isolated cyber-world, and the ability to visit her dad's grave by herself so that she could remember the good times they'd had together. Only these healing steps could create Megan's pathway toward freedom from pornography.

What's Real for Tammy

When Tammy explained that she justified viewing pornography in her hotel room as a way of avoiding being picked up in the lobby bar, I asked why *either* had to take place. Why was one of these scenarios bound to happen? Why couldn't she watch regular television, do a workout video, Skype with her family, or read a good book? That's when Tammy realized that she used sexual arousal as stress relief. If she couldn't have sex at home with her husband, which she confessed wasn't happening a whole lot anyway, and she wanted to avoid hooking up with a stranger, then watching porn and masturbating seemed to be the only option.

"So if stress relief is the ultimate goal, what is the source of your stress?" I inquired. "And how early in your life do you recall feeling similar pressures?"

Tammy launched into a tirade about how she had to work sixty hours a week to provide for their family of five. Because her husband's truck-driving salary wasn't nearly as much as her executive salary, they had mutually decided he would be the stay-at-home dad and she would bring home the bacon. But the arrangement was wearing on Tammy. She recalled being raised by a single mom who was always either at work or too tired to do anything once she came home. Tammy didn't want to be "that mom." But instead of sharing her feelings with her husband and asking him to help shoulder the financial load, she was escaping into her own fantasy world—a world where couples could "get it on" without the stresses of life, careers, and kids weighing them down. Of course, entertaining this fantasy wasn't helping her energy level as a mom, and it was robbing her of every ounce of sexual energy for her marriage.

I wondered if Tammy was giving her husband full credit for the countless hours he was investing in their family (no different than stay-at-home moms) or unconsciously blaming her husband for her dad's deadbeat approach to parenting and providing for a family. When I posed the question, Tammy stated, "Guilty as charged." We explored how their current family arrangement was created *by choice*, not *by force*, such as in the case of her own mom. And she could choose to change it at any time. Her husband was willing and able to work if necessary.

Tammy recognized how she had chosen to let stress get the best of her, and she was determined to take "her best" back for the sake of her family. She began having sex with her husband more often, especially before business trips. She spent more time on the phone with her children in the evenings, even having "Skype dinners" during extended trips. She took up Pilates and found books she enjoyed. She discovered these activities to be far more stress relieving than watching porn alone in her hotel room and wallowing in guilt afterward.

> Healing the world's pain begins with healing our own.

Our sexuality is as unique as our fingerprints. We all have different life stories and different images that float our sexual boats for whatever reason. Therefore, our fantasies will never fall neatly into a collection of boxes we can label as easily as the products adorning the pages in a Container Store catalog. I wish I could tell you, "If you fantasize about A, then B is always true, and if you fantasize about X, then Y is always true." Oh, if exposing the deeper meaning behind our sexual thoughts were only that easy!

> Scott Smith, age twenty-nine, was addicted to porn for two years. He explains, "Porn messes with the way you think of women. You want the women you are with to be like the women in porn. I was scared to get involved in a relationship. I did not know how extensive the damage was. I did not want to hurt anyone. I kept away from women."[10]

Fully understanding a fantasy or a particular bent toward specific images can only be accomplished *by the one doing the fantasizing*. A book can't interpret your fantasies for you, but *you* can. You know more about yourself and your own sexual thoughts than anyone else ever will, so again, my prayer is that this book equips you with the tools you need to connect the dots, reveal the bigger picture of why you fantasize the way you do, and successfully move your mind toward the high road of recovery.

THE REAL REMEDY

As Mitch, Megan, and Tammy's stories reveal, there is usually some sort of deep-seated emotional pain driving our pursuit of pornography. It is not that voyeurs of pornographic images are sick, twisted, or perverted. It is that they have an incredible dis-ease going on. They are uncomfortable in their own skin, in their own reality, and they don't know how to change that reality to make the dis-ease go away.

The key to healing from the dis-ease of voyeurism is to stop looking at other people to numb your pain and look directly into the pain itself. Before you click that mouse, call that phone sex hotline, or walk into that strip club, ask yourself, "What am I really feeling? When have I felt this way before, and why? Will what I'm about to do actually scratch my itch for relief from my dis-ease, or will it only make it worse?" Whether you are willing to seriously (and repeatedly) consider these questions is going to determine whether you stay entrenched in addiction or break free.

Our painful feelings must be processed. Swept under the rug, unresolved pain multiplies exponentially, giving birth to even more overwhelming feelings of guilt, shame, self-loathing, depression, anger, and bitterness, which drive us toward more self-numbing activities. However, brought out into the light where it can be carefully examined and understood, emotional pain can reveal what still needs to be "made right" in our minds. Embracing this healing journey can be scary at first but will eventually elicit feelings of acceptance, wholeness, gratitude, victory, and even great joy. As the apostle Paul wrote:

> We are full of joy even when we suffer. We know that our suffering gives us the strength to go on. The strength to go on produces character. Character produces hope. And hope will never let us down. (Rom. 5:3–5 NIRV)

Also consider how Jesus said, "They are blessed who grieve, for God will comfort them" (Matt. 5:4 NCV). In other words, it is a *blessing* to grieve our losses and to process our emotional pain. Going *there* is far more productive than turning to pornography.

Whereas pain is debilitating, healing is intoxicating. Try it. You may get hooked.

BEHIND THE CURTAIN: FROM PAIN TO PLEASURE TO PAIN AGAIN

As we have discussed, sexual arousal is an incredible tranquilizer for all kinds of emotional pain. The brain isn't capable of experiencing the height of sexual pleasure and the depth of emotional pain simultaneously, and because we naturally prefer pleasure, our brains devise a way to push all of our pain, anxieties, and insecurities aside—at least long enough to experience enough pleasure to climax.

Dr. Michael J. Bader, author of *Arousal: The Secret Logic of Sexual Fantasies*, explains the brain's uncanny ability to move beyond intense pain to experience intense pleasure:

> While our [hunger] and capacity for pleasure are instinctual, the road to pleasure is a complicated one. Our families and culture place numerous obstacles along this road: guilt, worry, fear, shame, rejection, and identification all stand in the way of getting to what seems so natural. It is an extraordinary testament to the creative and adaptive capacity of the human imagination that it is able to weave together exactly the right story to overcome obstacles to arousal. Getting turned on involves transcending the past, counteracting dangers, disconfirming beliefs, undoing traumas, soothing pain, and finally, finally, laying claim to pleasure.[11]

The fact that God wired our brains in such a magnificent way is a true testament to His love for us. He obviously longs for us to enjoy the physical pleasure He designed humans to experience. But there is one caveat: sexual ecstasy is only half-baked when we divorce physical pleasure from emotional connection, such as when we selfishly strive for orgasm through pornography and masturbation, rather than cultivating sexual ecstasy with our marriage partner. Love and relational intimacy are the yeast that allows our sexual ecstasy to rise to its highest level.

As one becomes more addicted to pornography and "solo sex," rather than "relational sex," he or she may find it increasingly difficult to experience sexual pleasure with his or her partner. This mental and physical condition is called *sexual anhedonia*.

Dr. Archibald Hart, author of *Thrilled to Death: How the Endless Pursuit of Pleasure Is Leaving Us Numb*, explains why men (in particular) so often develop anhedonia because of the specific ways they pursue sexual fulfillment. He writes:

> [Sexual] distortions arise because, unwittingly, we learn to connect our adrenaline arousal system (which is an *emergency* system) with our normal sexual hormone arousal. In other words, we come to look for exciting extras for sexual stimulation. When, for example, you engage in risky or out of the ordinary sexual behavior, the release of adrenaline adds excitement.
>
> For instance, the early sexual experiences of most men occur when they masturbate while looking at a porn magazine. Many men report that they inadvertently found the magazine in their father's drawer or desk. Since there is an element of fear attached at being found out or doing something naughty, a massive surge of adrenaline floods the body, adding excitement to sexual feelings. The problem is that it gives your sexual feelings a tremendous lift. Adrenaline adds

> an element of excitement that is not normally present in sexual arousal—or at least it shouldn't be. After a while, men get used to this *extra* sexual excitement coming from doing something sexual that is risky, and soon it becomes a habit, even an addiction.
>
> It is this pairing of adrenaline with sexual arousal that is the major cause of sexual distortion in our day. The sexual-adrenaline connection also leads to sexual perversions, such as adding pain to sex (sexual sadism and masochism) and, most seriously, rape (a crime that produces high-octane adrenaline).
>
> . . . [L]ittle attention has been given to how male sexuality has been grossly distorted by this pairing of sex to adrenaline. . . . Unfortunately, women pay the price for this distortion.[12]

How painful to be mentally and physically incapable of pleasure from the simplest of sexual acts! It should be enough to have passionate love flowing freely between the two naked bodies of a husband and wife. When we have to throw in danger or porn or pain to get excited, we are robbing ourselves (and our mates) of the deepest, richest sexual experiences possible. As Dr. Hart states so eloquently, "The pot of gold is found at the end of the relationship rainbow—nowhere else. Sexual pleasure is ultimately all about the quality of your relationship with your partner."[13]

Maybe you are reading this and feeling cheated, angry, or scared. Perhaps pornography has created too much unhealthy *intensity* in your marriage bed and robbed you of the genuine *intimacy* that you crave. If so, I assure you there is hope.

Just as we can go from pain to pleasure back to pain again, we can also go from pleasure to pain back to pleasure again! With

God's help, we can choose to evolve, to grow, to mature . . . to heal. So read on as we continue exposing the deeper meaning behind some of the most common sexual distortions that prevent this healthy evolution from taking place.

5

Bartering with Our Bodies

As we wrestled ourselves into our buoyancy vests and air tanks, our scuba instructor explained, "Some of your depth gauges have directional compasses; others do not."

I looked at the gauge in my hand. One dial would tell me how much air remained in my tank. The other would tell me how deeply into the water I was diving. There was no third dial indicating north, south, east, or west. But I wasn't worried. We were diving in a one-hundred-acre lake, not a gigantic ocean. Surely a compass wouldn't be needed.

We also assumed that sunscreen wasn't necessary. After all, we'd be thirty feet under water most of the time. However, my scuba mask kept filling up with water, regardless of how many times I cleared it, and I spent a lot more time at the surface wrestling with my mask straps than I had bargained for. So my exposed forehead got a lot more sun than anticipated.

By late afternoon, my fins were giving me fits, rubbing blisters on my little toes. Unable to swim at full speed, I was holding everyone back. Between my not-so-airtight face mask, my sunburned forehead, and my toe blisters, I decided I'd call it a day and let my husband and kids continue across the lake without me.

Backstroking the half mile back to the dock would have been the easiest approach, but that would fry my forehead in the Texas sun even more, so I put my regulator in my mouth, sank my face into the water, and began freestyling slowly in that direction. Or so I thought. After several tiring minutes, I looked up, thinking surely the dock was just a few more feet away. But somehow I had managed to get turned around, and I was even farther away from the dock than when I'd started! I was exhausted by the time I finally reached shore.

Without a compass, it's easy to lose our bearings. Not just in water or on land but also in relationships. Rather than looking to bless others, we seek people who will shoulder our burdens, right our wrongs, medicate our emotional pain, and provide the attention and affection we crave.

This is exactly what we see in the book of Genesis, as Satan distorted healthy relationships by luring the following people into immoral acts of premarital sex, prostitution, and seduction:

- Shechem forced Dinah to have premarital sex (Gen. 34:2).
- Tamar prostituted herself to Judah (Gen. 38:12–23).
- Potiphar's wife attempted to seduce Joseph (Gen. 39:7).

Each of these biblical characters shows us that "bartering with our bodies" has come naturally to humans since the fall of man. But the questions beg to be asked:

- *What* are we bartering for?
- *Who* are we bartering with?

And an even more important question is:

- Does the person we're bartering with possess what we're searching for, or have we merely lost our bearings?

In response to the first question, many would say that men are looking for sex and women are looking for romance. But this ultimately boils down to desiring the exact same things—affirmation, acceptance, comfort, and security. Although it sounds cliché, truer words were never spoken: we all are looking for love. Many of us just have some very distorted images of what love looks like and where it can be found—mainly because our mental, emotional, physical, and spiritual compasses are not always as reliable as we think.

Based on my professional experiences as a life coach, as well as my personal experiences as a recovering sex and relationship addict myself (a journey I've written extensively about in the Every Woman's Battle series), there are four main directions/relationships that humans gravitate toward in search of the love we naturally long for:

- the mother figure
- the father figure
- the fountain of youth
- the spiritual idol

Before we venture into these directions, let's discuss two Latin words that will give great insight to *why* they mean so much to us. The Latin words for "soul" are *anima* and *animus*. One of the patriarchs of psychology, Dr. Carl Jung, applied these terms to describe the feminine soul-image that resides in men (*anima*) and the masculine soul-image in women (*animus*). At first glance this can seem backward. Shouldn't the feminine image be inside the woman and the masculine image inside the man? But surely you have heard of women who find the strength to "pick themselves up by the bootstraps" or men who have swept their wives off their feet because they've "gotten in touch with their feminine side."

Humans actually possess *both* masculine and feminine spiritual components, just as God does. Remember, God is neither exclusively male nor female but both. (We talk more about "Searching for the Softer Side of God" in the "Behind the Curtain" feature at the end of this chapter.)

Dr. Jung theorized that the *anima* and *animus* appear regularly in our dreams and fantasies and play a tremendous role in the development of our personal and interpersonal lives. In fact, I would also say they greatly influence our marriages and family relationships as well since balancing masculine and feminine energies is something that parents unconsciously role-model for their children. Women often dream or fantasize about masculine images and men about feminine images.

By projecting their *anima* and *animus* images onto another person, both men and women often try to complete themselves through another (usually opposite-sex) human being. But the fantasy that another person holds what we are looking for is an absolute fallacy—one that has destroyed many lives and marriages. What we are looking for cannot be cultivated from another human being. It can only be cultivated, with God's help, inside ourselves.

Leanne Payne, author of *The Broken Image*, gives insight as to why cannibals eat other humans. They don't eat just to fill their tummies. They eat someone they perceive has characteristics and qualities that they are missing and that they would like to possess.[1] But, of course, having someone for dinner doesn't imbue *us* with *his* personality traits. Neither does being in a romantic relationship with that person. Yet how often do we see this type of mental bartering taking place?

- She's really uninhibited . . . so perhaps I can let go of all my inhibitions with her.
- He's famously brilliant . . . so if I'm his partner, people will think I'm smart too.
- She's stunningly gorgeous . . . so if she's on my arm, I'll look that much better.
- He's incredibly compassionate . . . I need more of that in my life, so I need *him*.

With this understanding of how our human psyche works, these four common (mis)directions will make a lot more sense.

ARE YOU MY MOTHER?

Perhaps you noticed in the last chapter that all three of our pornography "experts" struggled with "mother wounds" from childhood. Indeed, a secure attachment to our primary caretakers—usually our moms—is vital to our appropriate sexual development.

You may remember P. D. Eastman's classic story *Are You My Mother?* It's about a little bird searching high and low, mistaking everything from kittens and cows to boats and bulldozers, in search of the mama he longs to reconnect with. While there is certainly something in all of us that draws us toward a nurturing mother figure, many men search high and low to either (a) find a woman just like dear old Mom or (b) find a woman who can assure him that not *all* women are like his own mother, nor will *all* women make him feel the way his mother made him feel.

Ricardo will attest to this latter fact. At a Celebrate Recovery meeting Ricardo shared from the stage how every time he had sex with a woman (he estimated having more than one hundred partners within a thirty-year span of time), he was subconsciously screaming, "See, Ma! Somebody really does care about me! Somebody thinks I'm worthy of love!" But that feeling never lasted long before *she* ripped his heart out and stomped on it too. Ricardo realized that this approach to relationships worked about as well as drinking poison with the hope that someone else will die. It wasn't hurting his alcoholic mother. It was hurting the women he was trying to love and hurting him even further. He finally drew the conclusion that he had to stop bartering with his body, take a big step back from relationships altogether, and heal the mother wound that no other woman on the planet could possibly heal. He did this through extensive group and individual therapy, where he learned to nurture himself emotionally in the very ways he thought only another woman could.

Men are not the only ones who sometime need to "reparent" themselves. It is a skill women also must learn so that they do not go to unhealthy extremes in . . .

FILLING THE FATHER-SHAPED HOLE

If I had to identify the most common thread among all of my female clients who struggle with inappropriate sexual or emotional entanglements, it would be "unresolved daddy issues."

Just as a mother teaches her son how to properly interact with women, it's a father's job to teach his daughter that she is *worthy* of love, attention, and affection, not because of how she looks or what she'll do for him, but simply for who she is. If a girl doesn't get this gift from daddy in her formative years, she will be tempted to pound the pavement looking for it the rest of her life. She will concoct fantasy after fantasy of being found desirable by men. For example:

- Necia, who fell head over heels for her college roommate's father because he would visit often, lavishing the kind of attention on her that Necia only wished her dad was capable of expressing.
- Tina, who, by her own admission, dressed like a call girl throughout her teenage and college years because she saw how her father sexualized women and she was desperate for him to notice her somehow.
- Kelly, who was never able to say no to her controlling and critical father, allowed a ten-month sexual affair to develop between her and her boss. "I didn't want to make him feel rejected, nor did I want his wife to reject him, so I carried the load of guilt and shame for us both," she recalled.

Some women don't wake up to the fact that they are being codependent with a father figure until after the shine wears off of the relationship to reveal a very dysfunctional dynamic. Like Belinda, who at twenty-six married a man nineteen years her senior. "He made me feel safe, protected, and cherished," she explained. When they turned forty-five and sixty-four, respectively, she was hitting her sexual peak while he was on the downhill slide. Belinda admitted, "Even though he totally lit my fire for the first few years of our marriage, there's not a lot of sexual energy left. I feel more like I'm caring for my father than growing old with my lover. Father figures are fun until they turn into grandfather figures."

Of course, many of these father figures were actually just . . .

SEARCHING FOR A FOUNTAIN OF YOUTH

Perhaps you've heard the joke about the man who trades in his cold fifty-year-old wife for two hot twenty-five-year-olds. Or you've seen the movie *The Graduate* about Mrs. Robinson, a middle-aged mom, who seduces a twenty-one-year-old virgin. Searching for a younger sexual partner to hide the fact that we are growing older isn't the focus of just jokes and movies. It is frequently the stuff that headline news is made of as well, such as the forty-something youth pastor who wants to marry a fourteen-year-old member of his youth group, or the female teacher who is fired for having sex with one of her teenage students. Stories such as these give rise to terms such as *dirty old man*, *cougar*, and *midlife crisis*.

The label *cougar* is what motivated one woman (Alison) to connect with me. The word alone drove her crazy. In her early forties, Alison had Botox and breast implants to assuage her fears of losing her sex appeal as she aged. But she didn't expect that men half her age would take such overt notice of her new figure. She became chummy with a nineteen-year-old whom she worked with at a posh hotel, and she wasted a lot of brainpower wondering if he had sexual feelings toward her. (Her energies would have been more wisely invested examining whether *she* had sexual feelings toward *him*.) One night they were working a banquet together at the hotel. Toward the end of the evening, she dismissed all of the workers except this nineteen-year-old boy. Once it was just the two of them, it was "game on" in his mind. Immersed in a whirlwind of emotional heat and hormones, they wound up in one of the hotel rooms together after the banquet concluded. In the beginning, Alison minimized the interlude in her mind. *My husband isn't attentive enough. And he probably does the same thing when traveling.* Afterward, Satan maximized the encounter: *What a slut and a cougar you are! People can see right through you!*

Given that the fantasy of having a much younger sex partner is relatively common to both men and women, let's consider possible meanings behind this archetypal image. The most obvious reason is that society celebrates and glamorizes the firm bodies and energetic souls of young people far more than the passion, wisdom, and experience of older people. We have been conned by the media into believing that we lose our appeal as we grow older, but beauty is in the eye of the beholder. Plenty of people find aging men and women sexually attractive. There have actually been studies proving that both genders find gray hair particularly alluring.

The main reason Hollywood focuses its lens on youth is that young people are more exhibitionistic and easier to catch on film. Teens and twenty-somethings don't know any better than to lift their T-shirts for a *Girls Gone Wild* camera crew. They are still searching for their own sense of self and make easier targets for sexual exploitation.

An even deeper layer that we need to acknowledge is that as we age, our spouses age, too, and the question often looms large in at least one partner's mind, *Is this the beginning of the end of our (my) sex life?* Because sex appeal and arousal are often mental measuring sticks for vitality and quality of life, such a notion can be very scary. The thought of tapering off sexually can feel like slipping one foot into the grave and greasing the bottom of the other shoe. After all, we grew up thinking our own parents never had sex (they seemed *too* old for that!), and *none* of us ever envisioned our grandparents still having sex at their age (although many of us were quite wrong).

This fear of growing old and losing our mojo is what often drives middle-aged men to fantasize about their young receptionists or to mentally compare their wives to much younger women, thinking of all the ways their bodies don't measure up any longer. This is a very unfair comparison. Age happens to both of us (in equal proportion) as calendar pages turn. Her facial wrinkles, saggy breasts, and cellulite ripples don't have to be any less appealing to him than his receding hairline, belly paunch, and ever-growing nose and ear hair are to her. It's not about looking like Barbie and Ken dolls all our lives. It's all about loving each other and remaining as sexual as possible as we grow old together.

Let's trace this desire for a fountain of youth all the way down to its core. Why would we want to remain young and vibrant? So we can live forever or at least as long as possible. And where does this desire for eternal life come from? I believe it's woven into the fiber of our spiritual DNA because *eternal life is our inheritance through Christ.* There is so much wonder and delight that we can anticipate in heaven. This earthly life is merely a sad preview that pales in comparison.

So let's focus on investing wisely, making generous, eternal spiritual deposits into other people's lives (rather than worrying about being found sexually attractive) until Jesus returns.

Speaking of our spiritual DNA, let's dive into the final direction we often gravitate toward—spiritual idols.

BE STILL AND KNOW THAT YOU ARE MY GOD!

The main reason that we barter with our bodies for the attention and affection we deeply desire is that we don't trust God for the satisfaction we seek, the provision we need, or the comfort we crave. Why? Because it's much easier to reach for the middlemen (or middlewomen). They are readily available and eager to hold our projection screens while we play our mental movies onto them. God doesn't seem nearly as easy to access. But the truth is that He's more accessible and more eager to meet our needs than any human can be. We are just too spiritually lazy to look past the middlemen and seek the Real Deal.

But there is a tremendous difference between what a human has to offer and what God has to offer. So many women have discovered this reality the hard way. The possibility of passion and the notion of romance keep us captivated to the core, which is why romance novels and chick flicks are such a booming industry. We fantasize about being wooed and pursued by the perfect man who's been looking his whole life to find and fulfill a woman just like us—a wonderful, generous, considerate, and compassionate man who will move heaven and earth just to be with us! A man who'll lay down his life to protect us and provide for us, who'll bring out the very best in us and take great delight in us even on our worst days!

And why might a woman search the world (and the Internet) to find him? Because we've lost sight of the fact that we already have such a Man in our lives! His name is Jesus. No other man could possibly shoulder such burdens and live up to such expectations!

Women are certainly not the only ones in danger of adopting an opposite-sex archetype as a false god. Men are just as guilty, just as prone to this fantasy fallacy that a certain human being can fulfill our deepest longings.

A few years ago I received an anonymous e-mail from a pastor. He'd just read both *Every Man's Battle* and *Every Woman's Battle,* and he said he needed to confess his sin to someone who would understand. His fear was that his denominational leaders would certainly not be sympathetic. My guess is he was right.

He admitted to having four affairs over the previous ten years, all with women in his congregation:

> Each time these relationships started in my counseling office, as they bemoan the fact that their husbands aren't good spiritual

> leaders. They want men who will pray over them, discuss the Bible with them, draw them closer to God—all things that a pastor focuses his time and energy doing. So, of course, these women have seen me as a "direct connection" to God. I can't tell you how heady this is for a man to realize that a woman views him in such a way, especially when his wife belittles him at home. It's jolting . . . humbling . . . overwhelming . . . and yes, intoxicating. I always thought that these needy women were just looking for a man to be Jesus with skin on for them, and I was happy to oblige. But my flesh eventually got in the way every time. What I've come to understand is that *I wasn't just their god; they were, in fact, mine.*[2]

Whether we are male or female, we all must realize that fulfillment isn't found in another human being, no matter how appealing that other person may be, no matter how soothing and invigorating his or her presence may feel. Instead of looking to another, it's time to correct our compass and look to our Creator instead.

CORRECTING OUR COMPASS

Once we wake up from the fantasy that fulfillment can be found in a spiritual idol, a mother figure, a father figure, or a fountain-of-youth figure, we are ready to reach in the *right* direction. We are finally able to grasp the reality that what we are actually looking for can be found primarily in God and secondarily in ourselves.

Timothy Keller sheds light on this spiritual illumination process in his book *Counterfeit Gods*, where he explains:

> [Our fantasies and false idols sometimes] come crashing down around us. This is a great opportunity. We are briefly experiencing "disenchantment." In the old stories, that meant that

> the spell cast by the evil sorcerer was broken and there was the chance to escape. Such times come to us as individuals, when some great enterprise, pursuit, or person on which we have built our hopes fails to deliver what (we thought) was promised. . . .
>
> The way forward, out of despair, is to discern the idols of our hearts and our culture. But that will not be enough. The only way to free ourselves from the destructive influence of counterfeit gods is to turn back to the true one. The living God . . . is the only Lord who, if you find him, can truly fulfill you, and if you fail him, can truly forgive you.[3]

With this knowledge planted firmly in our brains, we can grasp the concept that "enchantment" with another human being is merely illusion, fantasy, wishful thinking, and misdirected projections.

Disenchantment, however, is the process of embracing an empowering reality. It's coming up to the surface of the water to get our bearings rather than swimming around in circles, thinking we're heading for home when we're really lost at sea.

What we often desperately search for in others, *we already possess* in God and in ourselves. Because God loves us, we can learn to love ourselves and others. Because God comforts us, we can comfort ourselves and others. Because God provides for our every need, we're able to stand on our own two feet and help others do the same. We can see someone who fits our mold, and instead of drawing that person into our emotional void and making an idol out of him or her, we can sit with

> "If I find in myself a desire which no experience in this world can satisfy, the most probable explanation is that I was made for another world."[4]
> —*C. S. Lewis*

that feeling. We can let the feelings swirling around inside us become inspiration for praise—"Thank You, Lord, for making such fine art!"—and choose to worship the Creator rather than the creation.

Embracing disenchantment with humans and enchantment with God alone allows us to grow up, put on our big-girl panties or our big-boy boxers, and be the responsible, spiritually mature adults that God created us to be. Instead of fantasizing about another person meeting all of our needs and bartering with our bodies for the attention and affection we crave, we're able to pay attention to the genuine needs of others and express affection toward our loved ones in healthy, holy ways.

BEHIND THE CURTAIN: SEARCHING FOR THE SOFTER SIDE OF GOD

My mom spent most of her career as a salesclerk at Sears, Roebuck and Co., so we not only had stock in Sears but also had Kenmore appliances throughout the kitchen and laundry room and Toughskins jeans in our closets.

So I clearly remember when Sears introduced a new marketing campaign with the slogan "Come See the Softer Side of Sears." The store wanted to make consumers aware that they weren't just about Craftsman tools and DieHard batteries but also about little black dresses, sleek heels to go with those dresses, and jewelry and purses. Sears wasn't just a "man's store" but a place where both men *and* women could shop for whatever they needed.

I'd like to start a similar campaign with the slogan "Come See the Softer Side of God!" We have grown up knowing that God is great at fighting battles and slaying enemies and doing all sorts of hard, manly tasks, but do we recognize that He is equally good at being soft? Can we sense God scooping us up to take comfort in His lap, gently brushing our tears away, or enveloping us in a warm embrace?

Unfortunately we often equate softness exclusively with femininity, and since our God paradigm is so masculine, it's hard to fathom God being the feminine nurturer we often crave. So what do we do when we (falsely) assume that God doesn't possess the softness that we crave? We naturally gravitate in the only direction we know to look—toward women—in the only way we know how—sexually.

You'd have to be hiding under a rock not to notice how much our culture idolizes the female body. I'm not saying that there's nothing sexy about the male physique, but most men acknowledge that their bodies pale in comparison to those of women. Without women willing to take their clothes off, the porn industry would fold. We have elevated the image of the sexy woman (think Marilyn Monroe, Beyoncé Knowles, and Kate Upton) to goddess status, and society bows down to that image (and many others like it) with time, attention, money, and sexual energies.

And there appears to be something that magically draws men (and women) in the direction of the sensuous female image. I believe there are two reasons for this supernatural pull: our longing for connection with the softer side of humanity and our longing for connection with the softer side of God.

We are hardwired as human beings to want closeness with a female because of the familiarity she represents. Life can be likened to a quest where we can only make sense of the journey by returning to our original destination. For humans this equates to a fascination with orgasm and the female body, for that *is* where we originated. As a result of orgasm, we are conceived, and our *first* experiences take place not in a labor and delivery room but in the female uterus and vagina. The womb is our first home. No wonder the female genitalia are a mesmerizing mystery—to both men and women!

And the moment we emerge from that womb, we are immediately thrust . . . where? Not to the male breast but to the female breast. It becomes our new home, from which breakfast, lunch, and dinner flow. I was recently visiting a friend who'd just had a baby, and the baby's fussiness level revealed it was feeding time. The newborn squirmed and squealed relentlessly until her mom brought her to the breast, and then she relaxed completely, whimpering multiple sighs of relief and contentment. Our survival instincts make the connection that this soft, warm place is where comfort, security, and nourishment reside.

Therefore, future emotional cravings for comfort and fulfillment might naturally result in an overwhelming desire to *return* to the powerful mental image of the breast.

This desire is what drives many to distraction—looking at pornography, visiting topless bars and strip clubs, seeking a prostitute, a sexual affair, or a lesbian partner. But could there be an even deeper spiritual longing behind such sexual longings?

I believe so because we are also hardwired to desire intimate connection, not just with earthly softness but also with sacred softness—the side of God that represents femininity. Because both men and women are made in the image of God (Gen. 1:27), it is a reasonable conclusion that God is neither male nor female but *both*. He is the perfect combination of masculinity and femininity.

Since most denominations embrace a strictly masculine image of God, we only hear Him referred to as "Father," never as "Mother." This creates two psychological dilemmas. First, for the woman who was abused by her father or a significant male in her life, connecting with God as Father can feel like a dangerous proposition. She might feel safer connecting with God as a

Mother since mothers often paint a softer, gentler picture of God in our minds than our fathers do.

Second, for the man who longs for relational intimacy, where can he go? Most likely he has been culturally conditioned that only gay men turn to other men. And because, in his mind, God is a male figure, it is a challenge to make the mental, emotional, and spiritual connection that God is the source of the fulfillment he seeks. He naturally turns to *women* instead.

But women can't fulfill men any better than men can fulfill women. *Oh, we try.* But we are draining each other dry, growing more and more disillusioned with how the opposite sex can never measure up to our expectations or meet all of our emotional and sexual needs.

We weren't designed to fully complete each other, only to complement one another. We must look to God to complete us. This can be done only as we embrace not just the masculine side of God but also the feminine side.

If you are thinking this sounds more "new agey" than biblical, consider that the Hebrew word *shaddai* comes from the root word "breast," and one of the most common words for God, *El Shaddai* (used forty-eight times in the Old Testament), can be translated "many-breasted one."[5] In other words, God is not just the Father figure who protects and provides; He is also the Mother figure who nourishes and comforts. This is a God who *can* meet all our needs . . . if only we would let Him.

6

When "One Flesh" Isn't Enough Flesh

When I was a teenager, my parents asked if I wanted to tag along on a double date with them and their friends, Dwayne and Jean. Being a fifth wheel on one of your parents' double dates wasn't exactly my ideal way to spend a Saturday evening, but I had no other plans, and when I learned they were going to my favorite all-you-can-eat seafood buffet, I relented.

Dwayne was a local businessman who owned a piano store in downtown Greenville, Texas. He knew every other shop owner on the square and how business was going for each one.

While eating at this seafood restaurant, Dwayne mentioned several times how sad it was that the restaurant would probably be going out of business soon. My curiosity got the best of me after he brought this up a third time, so I asked, "Why can't they stay in business?"

"Because people are *greedy*!" he replied, squinting his eyes tightly and staring straight at me. "They lose money on their all-you-can-eat buffet because customers take *way more* than their share, and many stuff their bags full of food to take home too! They even steal the condiments right off the table! Can you believe how greedy that is?"

I glanced over his shoulder, where a sign on the wall gave credence to Dwayne's theory. BUFFET ITEMS ARE FOR DINE-IN ONLY. *Hmmm . . . people are greedy, and business owners suffer. How sad!* I thought.

The next morning my mother and I were at church, and as they began to pass the offering plate she reached to unzip her purse. Suddenly she slammed it closed, as if there was a jellyfish in there about to sting her or something. Her face went pale as she stared straight ahead, trying to process what she'd just seen. I pulled the purse out of her clutches and looked inside. It was stuffed with dozens of individually wrapped packages of crackers, ketchup, and tartar sauce, plus lots of french fries and hush puppies wrapped in napkins!

Eyes wide, I looked back at her, and at the exact same moment, the lightbulb came on in both of our brains. "Dwayne!" we silently mouthed to one another. Then we got so tickled over his little prank that we made the pew shake with our muffled laughter.

Although the joke was totally on us, Dwayne was right. People *are* greedy at times—and not just at all-you-can-eat buffets. Sometimes we are greedy and selfish in the bedroom. And society has gotten *very* creative about our sexual selfishness. If "one flesh" isn't enough flesh, one can broaden relational horizons in a variety of ways. The most commonly pursued path is through an extramarital affair, but other possibilities exist, especially in people's fantasies. In the human head there's not just cheating but also swinging, swapping, threesomes, and even orgies going on!

THE MORE THE MERRIER?

It may be shocking to learn that some people (including Christians) fantasize in this direction, but alas, 'tis true. Recall Brett Kahr's statistics, quoted earlier from *Who's Been Sleeping in Your Head?*

- About 90 percent of adults fantasize about someone other than the person with whom they are having sex.
- 41 percent imagine sex with someone else's partner.
- 39 percent fantasize about sex with a work colleague.
- 25 percent fantasize about celebrities.

In the same book, Kahr also states:

- 28 percent of women fantasize about sex with two men.
- 58 percent of women fantasize about sex with two women.[1]

According to other polls, men's top sexual fantasies include having threesomes and watching lesbians have sex with one another.[2]

As explained earlier, fantasies aren't usually about the faces that appear in our minds. They are about *us*. So we must consider the archetypes represented, the story line being projected, and the deeper meaning behind these mental movies. And because we are sexual creatures, these movies play in spite of our best efforts to keep them at bay.

Even if we do manage to successfully squeeze them out of our brains during our waking hours, they often creep into our dreams. From *NOVA*'s "What Are Dreams?" episode, I learned that our dreams are most often polygamous. In fact, according to Antonio Zadra, dream researcher at the University of Montreal, a woman's sexual dreams include someone other than her spouse 80 percent of the time, and a man's sexual dreams include an extramarital partner 86 percent of the time.[3]

So, far more often than not, our mental activities venture way beyond the healthy boundaries established for us in Scripture.

HOW DID WE GET HERE?

Of course, one flesh not being enough flesh isn't anything new. But have you ever wondered where the fantasy of being sexual with more than one person originated? Or who was the first that we know of to act on the fantasy?

The answer to the latter question is Lamech. Only six generations removed from Adam, we see the first polygamous relationship mentioned in the Bible in Genesis 4:19 when Lamech marries *two* women, Adah and Zillah.

The answer to the first question (where the concept of multiple sex partners originated), I believe is the devil's doing. Think about it. God designed marriage such that "a man shall leave his father and mother and be joined to his wife, and they shall become one flesh" (Gen. 2:24 NKJV). He didn't create several men and women and say, "Take your pick, ladies and gentlemen! Can't decide? Sample as many as you want!" Nor did He make any concessions for three or four or more people to temporarily unite and become one flesh.

This mathematical miracle of one + one = one is something only God Himself could have imagined and orchestrated. But, of course, Satan is never satisfied leaving God's creation alone. He wants to add twists and spins on things, and luring God's people into polygamous relationships was one of his first attempts at distorting God's perfect plan of sexual intimacy between *one* husband and *one* wife.

Never in history was this distortion clearer than in King Solomon's case. In 1 Kings 11:2–3 we read:

> The LORD had told the Israelites "You must not marry people of other nations. If you do, they will cause you to follow their gods." But Solomon fell in love with these women. He had seven hundred wives who were from royal families and three hundred slave women who gave birth to his children. His wives caused him to turn away from God. (NCV)

King Solomon is considered one of the wisest men who ever lived, but one has to wonder about the wisdom of a man who chooses to marry seven hundred women! And have three hundred concubines to boot! How ironic that *this* man—who had all the wives (and all the sex) he wanted—would write such words as:

> *Useless! Useless!*
> *Completely useless!*
> *Everything is useless. . . .*
> *Everything is boring,*
> *so boring that you don't even want to talk about it.*
> *Words come again and again to our ears,*
> *but we never hear enough,*
> *nor can we ever really see all we want to see.* (Eccles. 1:2, 8 NCV)

I think the wisest thing that we can glean from King Solomon is that *no lust is ever fully satisfied*, and not even having an entire harem of sex partners at your disposal is enough to satisfy a fallen human being. Unfortunately we all fit that fallen category.

Of course, there are laws in most countries banning polygamy, so actually having more than one spouse isn't an issue in our society. But having more than one sex partner—either in reality or in fantasy—is undeniably an issue. For example, regardless of the wedding bands on their fingers and their conservative spiritual beliefs, the inner thoughts of these men and women are far more polyamorous than most moral compasses allow:

- Patricia, thirty-two, admits that she is unable to experience orgasm without thinking of someone besides her husband and, lately, most often fantasizes about her chiropractor.
- Paul, fifty-five, wondered for years what it would be like to have a threesome with his wife and another woman.
- Andrew, thirty-six, confessed to his wife that he has masturbated to sexual fantasies of a mutual friend from church.
- Renee, forty-one, reconnected via Facebook with the father of her first two children and for months afterward played a mental movie of "maybe he was the one I should have wound up with after all."
- Glenn, sixty-two, recalls fantasizing along with his wife back in the seventies about "swapping spouses" with Lee Majors and Farrah Fawcett.
- Gloria, forty-eight, reports that her most common sexual fantasy—the one that she knows will "trip her trigger"—involves her as a patient in the hospital having an orgy with multiple doctors and nurses.

Although names have been changed, each of these individuals represents actual scenarios that have been brought into my coaching office. Some people did the right thing with their fantasies. Others weren't so wise. But before I reveal the rest of their stories, let's explore . . .

THE DEEPER MEANING OF MULTIPLE PARTNERS

The Christian knee-jerk response to the kinds of fantasies mentioned here could easily be judgmental and condeming, but I prefer to leave the judging up to God and use the brains He gave us to get to the root of *why* the human mind often ventures in this direction despite our monogamous morals and values.

As a result of much reading, research, interviews, and prayer, I believe there are several possible explanations, given what we know about the brain's role in sexual arousal. This list is certainly not exhaustive but just a start to many possible theories:

- *The "Coloring Outside the Lines" Theory.* Although Christian parents certainly mean well, we often create sexually repressive environments for our children to grow up in. And because all children eventually reach an age when Mom and Dad's morals and values come into question, sexual rules and roles are often questioned, too, perhaps with great skepticism. This process is necessary for them to adopt certain spiritual and sexual values as their own, rather than as merely an inheritance. Therefore, sometimes a fantasy about unconventional sex (such as with more than one partner) is our mental way of taking a walk on the wild side. Such is the brain's way of trying to heal itself from overidentification or codependency on parental figures.
- *The "Double Your Pleasure, Double Your Fun" Theory.* If you are over forty, you probably remember the Doublemint gum commercials, featuring the Doublemint Twins. This theory is the simplest: if you have *two* people pleasuring you sexually, it will feel *twice* as nice. Someone who felt deprived in some way as a child may gravitate toward this mind-set

of wanting more than his or her fair share in case there's not enough to go around in the future. This is the brain's way of trying to heal itself from fear of poverty or scarcity.

- *The "Irresistible" Theory.* Because we accumulate so many negative messages about our looks, our abilities, and our desirability (or lack thereof), we are living as hurt little boys and girls trapped inside grown men's and women's bodies. But if more than one person wants to be sexual with us simultaneously, that must mean we deserve to be loved and pleasured and that we are irresistible to some people, on some level. And as these others lose all sexual inhibition in our presence, it will feel safer to let go of our own inhibitions as well. Such is the brain's way of trying to heal itself from low self-esteem.
- *The "Too Much to Handle" Theory.* The notion that my spouse isn't enough to fully satisfy me is relatively common, especially among men (or women going through their sexual peak, typically in their forties). Having multiple sex partners, either individually or all at the same time, alleviates the fear that you are putting too much of a burden on one person. I believe this stems from growing up with parents who overtly or covertly sent us the message, "I don't have time or energy for you," which creates what feels like a Grand Canyon of emotional (and sexual) needs inside our spirits. Deep down, we assume that one human being can never fill the void, so we fantasize about having multiple people do it. Such is the brain's way of trying to heal itself from neediness.
- *The "Sharing the Load" Theory.* When engaged in sex with more than one partner, other people are present to handle the responsibility of providing pleasure to each participant. That way, it is no longer about personal

performance but about being a team player. This mentality is often a result of growing up feeling insecure about our own abilities to live up to other people's expectations, such as in the case of a child whose parent is an extreme perfectionist. This is the brain's way of trying to heal itself from performance anxiety.

- *The "It Ain't Gay if It's a Three-Way" Theory.* We can't ignore the fact that a fantasy of having multiple partners simultaneously often equates to sexual thoughts that are both heterosexual and homosexual in nature. If you have three people but only two genders, then someone's doing something with someone of the same sex. We will explore homosexual fantasies in the next chapter, but in this context I believe the fantasizer is mentally creating a more socially acceptable context for exploring his or her homosexual curiosities. This is the brain's way of trying to heal itself from identity confusion or guilt over desiring what is considered socially and spiritually taboo.
- *The "Closest Thing to Heaven" Theory.* I've given much thought and prayer to why anyone (especially Christians) would ever find the thought of a group orgy sexually arousing. I truly believe that underneath every sexual desire is an even deeper spiritual desire, and when I think of what heaven will be like, I envision complete unity, harmony, and love unlike anything we have experienced here on earth among fallen creatures. I also envision extreme intensity, as we'll never get bored in heaven. Aren't these the very feelings that we are trying to create in our minds when we envision an orgy? (Granted, it's infused with the twisted sexual distortions that have been passed down to us since Genesis.) A group of people with similar goals, desires, and passions, all uniting in harmony to bring

great intensity and delight to one another, could possibly be someone's (sexual) way of envisioning what heaven really will be like. If so, this is most likely the brain's way of trying to heal itself from the disillusionment and disappointment of broken relationships.

In the book *False Intimacy: Understanding the Struggle of Sexual Addiction*, Dr. Harry Schaumburg explains:

> A sexual fantasy stems from a desire to gain more in a relationship than is possible. It's an attempt to gorge ourselves with passion and move into a state free of any chance for disappointment. Simply put, we want to enter the Garden of Eden again.
>
> But the very desire to know the bliss of the Garden here on earth is skewed by our obsession with self. In demanding the bliss of someone's real or imagined warmth, we become consumed with ourselves, which destroys the very ecstasy we seek. There is no way out. We are locked in reality, always wanting and therefore always destroying what we want. The process is insane. Until we become consumed with the love that desires to give for the sake of another's good, all joy is an illusion.[4]

Again, we could develop many more theories in addition to these, but the common thread is that sexual fantasies are the brain's way of trying to heal itself from emotions that aren't compatible with climax. We must somehow clear our minds of "stinking thinking" and compartmentalize our pain long enough to experience the heightened sense of pleasure we naturally desire.

I don't know about you, but I think that God's wiring of

the human brain with this ability is an absolute miracle and an extravagant gift for which I'm incredibly grateful.

But this gift can also leave us wrestling with the question . . .

DO FANTASIES MAKE GOOD REALITIES?

With a better understanding of the role our sexual fantasies play, it is much easier to answer the question, "Is this what we *really* want?" Do we actually desire multiple partners in reality or strictly in our minds? Let's return to those individuals introduced earlier and discover how they answered these questions and the valuable lessons they learned:

> "He that cannot bear with other People's Passions, cannot govern his own."[5]
> *—Benjamin Franklin,*
> Poor Richard's Almanack

- Patricia realized that just because someone comes into your mind when you are sexually aroused doesn't mean you're being unfaithful. She commented, "I don't feel the need to fantasize about my husband because he's right there with me." She also figured out a likely explanation behind her chiropractor fantasy; fortunately it was before she spoke up about it to the doctor and made a fool of herself or opened up an awkward can of worms. She recalls her mother taking her at least once a year for an adjustment, but she felt traumatized by the doctor's gruff exterior and rough hands. Her new chiropractor, however, is the antithesis of the one she had as a child. He is young, handsome, and friendly and has a more gentle approach. She merely feels more at ease than ever before and is letting her mental guard down from the "extreme fear" position she had as a child.

- After years of encouraging his wife, Theresa, to keep her "radar up" for a potential threesome partner (partly in jest, partly not), Paul got his wish. Only it backfired. Theresa says she caved in to his numerous requests as a last-ditch attempt to save their struggling marriage. Although he assumed the experience would lead them to new levels of passion and pleasure and scratch his itch, he was left scratching his head. It seemed Theresa preferred this woman *over* him, both in and out of the bedroom. He was left on the sidelines during most of the encounter, experiencing the sting of rejection from not just one but *two* women simultaneously, which was a major blow to his ego. Then Theresa began spending most evenings and weekends with this other woman. Their marriage didn't survive when Theresa decided to leave him and embrace her new lesbian lifestyle.
- When Andrew confessed to his wife that he had masturbated to a fantasy of a female friend, his intentions were pure. He had never acted on his fantasies, but he truly felt horrible and wanted to absolve himself of the guilt. The problem was that his wife grew up in a home where her father was unfaithful to her mother, and this news flash ripped the scab right off that wound. She assumed Andrew was headed in the same direction and wanted to do everything she could to prevent that. She demanded that he make a list of every single woman he had ever fantasized about, so she could make sure none of these women ever came around. Andrew was mortified at her extreme response but complied out of desperation to quell her anger, although she still seems angry years later. He admits, "I know I shouldn't have fantasized about another woman in the first place, but had I known what

this would do to my wife and marriage, I'd have chosen a different accountability partner for sure."

- When Renee reconnected with her first husband via Facebook, she was attempting to heal wounds both of them had suffered from a bitter divorce years earlier. What she didn't bargain for, however, was that some rough emotional and financial times in her second marriage caused her to fantasize about that "green grass on the other side of the fence" she once enjoyed. She did meet up with him in a hotel "for old time's sake," and they had sex, which turned out to be incredibly anticlimactic when he rolled over and went right to sleep afterward. She lay for hours in knots over what she had just done and worried about the impact it would have on her second marriage. Renee spewed, "The reality of being with him again wasn't nearly as good as the fantasy! I wish I'd just let that sleeping dog lie." Then she continued, "Well . . . I guess I kind of did, but not as fast as I should have."
- When Glenn saw Farrah Fawcett giving an interview with husband Lee Majors, he pointed to Farrah and joked to his wife, "I'd risk my marriage for that!" Fortunately she was a good sport about it, pointed to Lee Majors, and bantered back, "I'd risk my marriage for *that*!" Of course, they never acted on this fantasy in any way. It actually became an inside joke between them, and every time *Charlie's Angels* or *The Six Million Dollar Man* came on television, they both knew there would be some sexual sparks between them! They learned that it's not necessary to take their spouse's (or their own) celebrity fantasies too seriously.
- Gloria's hospital orgy fantasy disturbed her for decades, and she finally confessed it to her husband after twenty years of marriage. He was actually the one who helped

> her make a connection between her sexual present and her distant past. "Weren't you in the hospital for a long time when you were a little girl?" he asked. Indeed, when Gloria was eleven years old, she and her mother spent three weeks in separate hospital rooms after a very serious car accident. Gloria remembers this to be an incredibly scary time, but the doctors and nurses were so comforting with all of their jokes and expressions of compassion and concern that she grew very fond of several of them. "No wonder that's where my brain gravitates when I want to relax, feel safe, and be pleasured!" she realized.

It's a wonder how the human brain creates intimate connections with certain people, places, things, or sensations. No need to give ourselves forty lashes, run to confession, or wallow in guilt over a vivid sexual imagination. We can thank God that . . .

- our brains know how to compensate so well, turning emotional pain into erotic pleasure and traumatic burdens into treasured wisdom.
- He doesn't condemn us for mentally operating this way, for it's all a part of His divine human design.
- we can connect our own dots and make sense of our sexual thoughts, rather than trying to turn the fantasy into reality.

The Amazing Sexual Brain

Ever wonder what happens in the brain during sexual arousal and climax?

A team of scientists at the University of Groningen in the Netherlands did and conducted extensive research to reveal the answers. Using PET scans to monitor subjects while resting, while being sexually stimulated, and while having an orgasm, they discovered the following fascinating details:

- The area of the brain behind the left eye, the lateral orbitofrontal cortex, is the seat of reason and behavioral control. In both men and women this region shuts down during orgasm. That's what provides the out-of-control feeling that creates confusion but also produces intense pleasure.[6] (Perhaps orgasm is really our sovereign God's way of reminding us that we are not as in control as we think we are.)
- When you compare the brain of a person taking heroin and the brain of a person having an orgasm, they are 95 percent the same.[7] (Perhaps climax is God's way of providing a legal, inexpensive, and healthy way to get high.)
- Women's brains showed decreased activity in the amygdala and hippocampus, which control fear and anxiety. This could explain why women have more of a need to feel safe and relaxed in order to enjoy sex.[8] (Perhaps this is God's way of ensuring that *intimacy* is sought over *intensity* in a sexual relationship.)

Medical science proves once again that the more we learn about the human body and how it functions, the more we stand in awe of our magnificent Creator!

The need for comfort, safety, love, and intimacy in relationships is what sets us apart from the animal kingdom. If we were just bundles of hormones looking to hump anyone for sexual satisfaction, we'd be dogs, not humans.

But at least animals instinctively know that sex is intended for *two*, not three or four or more. You never see monkeys, manta rays, cows, or cockatoos having three-ways or orgies because it's just unnatural. So why do humans try to complicate something that's so simple? Why do we sometimes assume that the racy scenarios going on in our brains need to be played out in real life to provide satisfaction? I believe it's due to the fact that we don't realize where sexual satisfaction is truly found—in the power of the one-flesh union.

THE POWER OF "ONE FLESH"

If we are not careful, we can start believing that God is a supernatural killjoy who wants to rob us of pleasure by limiting our sexual partners. The reality is that God wants to *enhance* our pleasure by limiting our emotional pain. He knows that when two human beings experience sexual intimacy with one another, they form a tight emotional and spiritual bond—a bond that brings excruciating pain when it must be ripped apart.

Marriage is designed such that this painful separation *never* has to take place. Granted, there are many times when we hurt each other; then we talk it over and walk through the pain together and we heal together, and grow together. And throughout this sacred process, sex reinforces our relationship. This kind of sexual intimacy between spouses seeps deep into the fibers of our being, much more so than sex outside marriage. It's like the difference between superglue and Scotch tape. If our brains are looking for a sense of permanence, safety, and security in order to experience the highest of sexual highs, we need look no further than the person whose head is already on the pillow next to ours.

Seeing your spouse not just as a companion or roommate but as a sexual soul mate will require abandoning your fantasy version of intimacy and embracing the real deal. Genuine intimacy can best be defined by breaking the word into syllables: *in-to-me-see.* In other words, "I will let you see into the deepest parts of me without fear or hesitation. I will peer into the deepest parts of you without judgment or condemnation. I will love you as completely and unconditionally as I love myself."

With this mind-set you can become willing to offer your uninhibited self completely—looking past pains, warts, scars, blemishes, distorted mental fantasies and all. Don't feel as if you must get your act completely together before becoming vulnerable in the bedroom. Your spouse needs you *now,* just as you are, so that he or she can feel the freedom to be exactly who he or she is. As Gary Thomas, author of *Sacred Marriage,* explains:

> Continuing to give your body to your spouse even when you believe it constitutes "damaged goods" can be tremendously rewarding spiritually. It engenders humility, service, and an other-centered focus, as well as hammering home a very powerful spiritual principle: Give what you have.[9]

Once you are giving all that you have, you open your mental channels to receiving the very pleasures you are offering. But the giving has to come before the receiving. If you are in it for what you desire to *get* rather than what you desire to *give,* your spouse will automatically feel more like a sexual vending machine than an intimate partner.

Remember, we are multifaceted creatures, seeking satisfaction not just physically but also mentally, emotionally, and spiritually.

Therefore, the goal of a one-flesh union is to create emotional and spiritual energy in the bedroom as much as it is to create physical pleasure. Thomas goes on to say:

> Sex is about physical touch, to be sure, but it is about far more than physical touch. It is about what is going on *inside* us. Developing a fulfilling sex life means I concern myself more with bringing generosity and service to bed than bringing washboard abdomens. It means I see my wife as a holy temple of God, not just as a tantalizing human body. It even means that sex becomes a form of physical prayer—a picture of heavenly intimacy that rivals the *shekinah* glory of old.
>
> Our God, who is spirit (John 4:24), can be found behind the very physical panting, sweating, and pleasurable entangling of limbs and body parts. He doesn't turn away. He wants us to run into sex, but to do so with his presence, priorities, and virtues marking our pursuit. If we experience sex in this way, we will be transformed in the marriage bed every bit as much as we are transformed on our knees in prayer.[10]

Spiritual transformation, mental healing, emotional wholeness, physical comfort and security, and enormous pleasure—these are the harvest fruits of sex according to God's perfect plan. These are the rewards of relishing our roles as husband and wife to one another.

As we lose ourselves, not in fantasy, but in the reality of sharing our innermost selves with God and with each other, we gain the deepest sense of satisfaction humanly possible. We experience what it means to truly be one flesh with both the Creator and His creation.

And not only is one flesh *enough* flesh, but it also can provide such an overwhelming sense of ecstasy that we ought to feel downright *greedy*!

Fortunately, thanks be to God, we don't have to.

BEHIND THE CURTAIN: BRENT'S "ROCK BOTTOM"

A nervous energy bounced off the walls of my coaching office as Brent and Arlene sat stiffly on my couch. They had come to see me because Arlene was having "trust issues" due to some of Brent's recent activities—activities revealing that one flesh hadn't been enough flesh for Brent.

I asked that one of them explain further about these activities, and Arlene expounded. "I found pornography on Brent's computer two years ago, and he promised me it would never happen again. To my knowledge it hasn't, but what he's done this time is far worse."

She went on to explain that she had discovered text messages and e-mails with a woman he had recently met at a conference and that some of these messages included nude photos and masturbation videos. "How can I trust him ever again?" she cried.

The truth was that Brent couldn't answer that question because he didn't know how he was ever going to trust *himself*. He'd struggled with sexual addictions for almost two decades, and quite frankly, he was sick of himself and his own behavior.

I met with Brent and Arlene several times over a six-month period, focusing on peeling back the layers of Brent's sexual addiction to discover some of the root causes. As I explained, "You can't change the fruit until you trace the root."

What I learned about Brent's life was heartbreaking, and I often wondered how many men would honestly say their stories are similar if they knew the details. I also wondered how many women could see past their husbands' weaknesses to their genuine emotional needs if they only knew the whole story behind their addictive behaviors.

I asked Brent to start by telling me about his family of origin. As the baby of the family, he had a close relationship with his mom, but his older brothers chastised him for it, calling him a "mama's boy." His brothers were so much older that he didn't have much of a relationship with them. Brent described his dad as "emotionally unavailable because he was always at work or drunk." He also recalled his father disciplining him unfairly. He described his primary feelings toward his father as *fear* and *disrespect*.

Brent almost broke down in tears when he deduced, "I hated my father for all these reasons, yet here I am, acting just like him! I can't seem to be faithful to my wife; I drown my sorrows by spending way too much time drinking with the people I work with; I take out my self-loathing on my kids and discipline them harshly; I fear what I'm capable of, and I'm the last person on the planet who deserves *any* respect from anyone!" It was during this session that Arlene's hard exterior cracked, and her anger toward Brent melted into sadness and sorrow.

As we explored Brent's first exposure to inappropriate sexual conduct, he explained that it began when he was seven years old and found his father's *Penthouse* and *Playboy* magazines under his parents' bed. "Seeing naked women sent a surge through my belly unlike anything I'd ever experienced, but I admit that it made me angry that my dad was looking at other women besides my mom. I couldn't imagine that she was okay with that, and it made me want to punch him in the stomach. Even at that age, I knew my mom deserved better, and I remember thinking that I would never want to make my wife feel bad like that." There was a long pause, and then Brent took Arlene's hand, looked directly into her eyes, and tearfully admitted, "But I have . . . in so many ways . . . and I can't tell you how sorry I am."

At ten years old, Brent walked outside his dad's shop to discover him and another woman leaning against the building and kissing passionately. When his dad saw that Brent had witnessed this scene, he smiled faintly, winked, and placed his index finger to his lips as if to say, "Shhhh . . . let's keep this to ourselves." It was then that Brent internalized the message that "secrets are okay for guys to have. It's just what men do."

At fourteen, Brent was pursued sexually by a nineteen-year-old girl. He recalled, "I didn't necessarily want to have sex yet, especially not with a girl I knew I could never even date, but I remembered 'this is just what men do,' and I desperately wanted to feel like a man, so I went through with it." Brent had never stopped to consider that he had lost his virginity to a statutory rapist. (Yes, women who sexually abuse underage boys are acting just as illegally as a man who does the same thing to an underage girl.)

I asked Brent if he knew how many sexual partners he'd had over the past twenty years since that first experience. He hesitated, ashamed of the number rolling around in his head. Arlene coaxed, "I promise it's not going to change how I feel about you. I just want you to be honest—not just with me but with yourself." He estimated that he had probably slept with about sixty or seventy women.

Recognizing that Brent was what women commonly refer to as "eye candy," I asked a follow-up question. "Of those women, how many would you say pursued *you* inappropriately, similarly to your first sexual experience?" He thought for several seconds and responded, "Probably ninety-five percent. I've never really *wanted* to have sex with any woman in particular except my first wife and Arlene [his second wife]. But the fantasy of being a 'real man' and being found 'desirable' to a woman led me to lower my guard and do some pretty stupid stuff that, quite frankly, I'm not very proud of. If *this* is what men do, I'm not sure I want to be one!"

Of course, Brent didn't have a choice about whether he was a man or not, but he did have a choice about what kind of man he wanted to be. We discussed at length whether or not he was ready to declare his most recent illicit behavior his "rock bottom." Indeed, Brent had no desire to descend any deeper into the depths of sexual compromise than he already had. He didn't want to hurt Arlene any further. He was ready to become the man he wished he had been all along.

We began cleaning out Brent's "relational refrigerator" of all the "stinky leftovers" from his childhood. Using index cards, a marker, and an empty Tupperware container, we discussed some of the lies he had believed about men, women, and sex. Lies such as:

- This is just what men do.
- It's okay for men to keep secrets from women.
- A real man gives women what they want, even if it's not what *he* wants.
- As long as I don't go "all the way," it's not cheating.
- If I do go all the way, what's one more time?
- Men need pornography (or naked photos or masturbation videos) for visual stimulation because looking at their wives isn't sufficient stimulus.
- You can drown your self-loathing from all your sexual misconduct in a few shot glasses full of whiskey.

I asked Brent what he wanted to do with this Tupperware container full of leftovers that had gone bad. Did he want to take it home and let them spoil his life even further or leave them with me in my office where they wouldn't burden him any longer?

I wasn't surprised that he chose to leave them behind. And Arlene was *delighted* to see him do so.

7

Grappling with Gay and Lesbian Fantasies

When I was invited to be one of the keynote speakers at an Exodus International Conference, I was honored . . . but hesitant. After searching for the root of my anxiety, I realized that I wasn't sure what kind of presentation to make to this particular audience. Exodus International is a ministry that focuses on equipping the church. Exodus also offers biblical guidance to individuals who are either dealing with or personally affected by homosexuality.

Not quite sure of what I had to offer, I finally decided to call the conference organizer, David, and be honest about my dilemma. I admitted, "I'm rather stumped as to what kind of message to craft. Are you aware that my testimony doesn't include anything about homosexuality?"

David replied, "Shannon, we don't want you to talk to us about homosexuality. We simply want you to be transparent, to share your personal story of sexual and relational struggles, along with how God helped you walk through your own process of healing.

Teach us God's intent for biblical sexuality and healthy relationships, what He desires for us all to enjoy with both the same and opposite sex!"

Now *that* I knew I could do. What I didn't know, however, was that I wasn't really going to teach. I was going to learn. Over a two-day period, I met some of the most wonderfully authentic people on the planet. There was no mask wearing, no posturing, no candy coating. No one hid his or her agenda in attending the conference. Many of the attendees once identified themselves as gay, but they didn't want to be bound to that identity or struggle any longer. They sensed that freedom was possible, and they came hungry to learn, to grow, and to heal.

It was one of the most receptive audiences I have ever encountered. But again, I learned as much as (if not more than) they did. And the biggest nugget of truth and wisdom that I walked away with was that homosexuality isn't just a cultural phenomenon or a social issue. After that conference, homosexuality had beautiful faces, names, and stories. Amazing stories.

NATURE VERSUS NURTURE

Before I share just a few of these people and their stories with you, let me make a disclaimer here. I know there is much debate about whether or not someone is born gay or culturally conditioned to become that way. The whole "nature versus nurture" debate has been going on even longer than I've been alive, and there are plenty of intelligent, respectable folks on both sides of this fence.

One is Louann Brizendine, a medical doctor and researcher and the best-selling author of a book called *The Female Brain*, in which she summarizes the following findings about the brains of both women and men:

- Same-sex attraction is estimated to occur in 5 to 10 percent of the female population.
- Men are twice as likely as women to be gay.
- Several family and twin studies provide clear evidence for a genetic component to both male and female sexual orientation.[1]

Based on Dr. Brizendine's research evidence, she believes that homosexuality is in some people's nature. Regardless of our theological views on homosexuality, we do not have enough scientific information to disprove this theory of some people being genetically predisposed to homosexuality.

Let's add to the mix other opinions, such as that of Cynthia Nixon, who starred for years on the television show *Sex and the City*. In an interview with the *New York Times*, she stated that she wasn't *born* gay, rather, "for me, it is a choice."[2] Another woman was recently on the radio talking about how she used to be a lesbian, but she's now marrying a man. She explained, "The gay community completely supported me as long as I supported their agenda. But now that I'm debunking their myth that 'if you're gay, you're gay; come out of the closet and stay that way,' well, they're not so supportive." Many men who attended the Exodus International Conference echoed this sentiment. As long as they chose to be with a male partner, they were celebrated. As soon as they chose to leave that partner to find a wife and start a family, they were ostracized. But the fact that some previously gay people *can* choose an opposite-sex partner and find great happiness and sexual fulfillment is evidence that, for many, it *is* a choice.

Making a case for the nature versus nurture argument is certainly not on my agenda. My burden for writing this chapter is to help (1) people who are struggling to either avoid or break free from homosexual relationships and (2) the many women and men who have experienced (and been bewildered by) homosexual fantasies, even though they consider themselves to be very heterosexual beings. People such as:

- Monica, who, in her thirties, fears that she might be gay because her sexual dreams always have involved women rather than men and she is unable to come to orgasm with her husband unless she mentally entertains lesbian fantasies.
- Charlie, who views gay male pornography and wrestles with the urge to visit a massage parlor where male prostitutes offer a variety of other "services."
- Gail, whose "masculine personality" led her to embrace a tomboy persona as a child and who has a bisexual identity as an adult.

There are many layers to homosexual fantasies. It is only as we peel back those layers, revealing more of the intimate details of an individual's life, that we are able to identify the real root of someone's sexual struggles.

PEELING BACK THE LAYERS

Understanding the deeper meanings behind homosexual fantasies is an incredibly complex process because our brains are incredibly complex creations. Contrary to popular belief, homosexuality isn't about what happens between a man's or woman's legs. It's about what happens between one's ears. And what happens between the ears most likely started long before puberty.

Monica's Mystery

Monica explained in our first session, "I deal with lesbian images while my husband is pleasuring me, and I hate this about myself! I feel really wrong for allowing these thoughts in my head. I have prayed and prayed for deliverance from this but still find it impossible to experience an orgasm any other way."

As we began unpacking Monica's earliest memories, she remembered her father frequently coming home from work in a foul frame of mind. "Everyone walked on eggshells when we knew Dad was in a bad mood!" she recalled. Occasionally her father would hit her mother across the face when arguments broke out, and Monica's two older brothers usually took her by the hand and headed toward the backyard to play outside when this happened. It was their way of escaping the chaos and protecting their little sister from further violent outbursts.

But one day when Monica was six and her brothers were ten and twelve, they failed to protect her—not from their dad, but from a neighbor boy. He suggested they play hide-and-seek. Monica would be "it" first, and she'd count to twenty while lying on the bed with a pillow covering her face. Monica complied, but instead of running away to hide while she was counting, the neighbor boy slid his hand up her dress and forced his finger into her vagina. She squirmed and tried to scream, but suddenly more hands held her down and the pillow was pressed harder against her face to muffle her voice.

Monica doesn't remember what happened next. Her brain obviously shut down to protect her from the gravity of the situation, but she distinctly remembers the horror of realizing that it was her own brothers who served as the neighbor boy's accomplices.

Eight years later, when Monica was fourteen and her oldest brother was twenty, he committed suicide. She has no idea if guilt over what happened that day played any role in his decision to end his life. But one idea she did develop throughout these tumultuous younger years was that men were incredibly dangerous. They were angry, mean, violent, abusive creatures who couldn't be trusted any farther than Monica could spit. Her father, her brothers, and her neighbor had all taught her well that girls were not safe in a boys' world.

Therefore, in order for Monica to ever feel safe enough in her own mental space to reach a sexual climax, she couldn't be in a boys' world where she still felt vulnerable to danger and violence. She had to be in an all-girls' world, where she was nurtured and safe.

Does this mean that Monica needs to leave her husband and succumb to the lure of lesbianism? Absolutely not. Her marriage to a man who respects and honors her, a husband who is tender with her sexually, has been one of the most healing relationships of her life. With her newfound understanding of where these lesbian fantasies originated, she feels more confident than ever that they only have as much power over her as she chooses to give them, which is very little.

Charlie's Father Hunger

I first met Charlie when he was a teenager at a summer camp I was directing. He kept in contact throughout his college years and is still a friend today. He is an amazingly talented young man who loves God and his wife deeply, but like many of us, he has his own sexual dragons to slay.

He discovered pornography when he was in sixth grade, and he considered himself a full-blown addict by the time he was a freshman in high school. He was disgusted with himself for gravitating most often to exclusively male pornography. Although he's never pursued a partner for a homosexual encounter, he has visited a male massage parlor, sometimes opting for more than just a back rub, other times refraining. "This is the one thing I hate about myself more than anything else!" he exclaims. "Why can't I be drawn just to women like a 'normal' guy?"

The reality is that there is no such thing as "normal" when it comes to sex. And when we peel back the layers of Charlie's childhood, his situation isn't difficult to understand. When he was three, his father left home, leaving Charlie to be raised by his manic-depressive mom. Throughout the next fifteen years his mom would often leave the house in a rage, threatening never to return. Sometimes she stayed out all night or was gone two or three days in a row. Rather than coming home from school to a mom and dad who provided unconditional love and unwavering support, he lived in constant fear that he had been abandoned or would be soon.

His anger and loneliness drove him toward Internet porn, where he found the scenarios that most appealed to him were raw images of men releasing their sexual aggression in unconventional, uninhibited ways. It was like releasing the steam valve on a pressure cooker, providing some semblance of relief, if only for a few minutes. But then the weight of guilt and confusion would sink in even heavier than the anger he was trying to release. It became a vicious cycle.

I asked Charlie to pay attention to those moments when he felt most tempted either to access pornography or revisit the male massage parlor. What was happening? How was he feeling? What was his perception of what he needed at that moment? And might there be a better, less guilt-inducing way to cope with the situation?

He realized that his draw toward men for a sexual release (through porn or massage) was strongest when he felt overwhelmed or inadequate at work. He explained, "My boss is a really smart guy, and I want to impress him. But when that becomes a challenge, I feel like a failure. I feel like that little boy who wasn't good enough to make his dad want to stick around and watch me grow up. And my mom taught me that women could never be fully relied upon. So I guess I'm wanting to run to another man to make *me* feel like a man—to fill the void my dad created when he left."

"Is there any man on the planet who can fill that void, Charlie? Can another human being really make you feel like a *man*?" I asked.

Tears flowed freely down Charlie's cheeks as he realized that he was chasing the intangible, pursuing the impossible. "No, but I don't know what else to do!" he sobbed.

"Who created you as a man, Charlie?"

"God did," he replied.

We went on to discuss what it would look like to let God heal the father-shaped hole in Charlie's heart, to let God show him how to reparent *himself* so that he has his own well of affirmation and strength that he can draw from as needed, to let God teach him what it really means to be a man, and to let God help him carve out a whole new path for effectively managing his stress and anxiety (through exercise, manual labor, meditation, healthy male friendships, and marital sex) so that he didn't have to keep trying the same fruitless things over and over again.

Charlie last reported that he hasn't surfed for porn or visited the massage parlor in over three years. He and his wife now have a son of their own, and he's determined to be the awesome dad he never had.

Gail's Gender Confusion

Gail suspected she was "different" when she was in junior high. Her teachers commented repeatedly, "You're as good at math and science as the boys!" Her PE coaches exclaimed, "We should make room for you on the sports teams, Gail! You throw a ball better than any boy in this school!"

Because she was very competitive and was intimidating to most male students, Gail wasn't pursued by the boys the way the other girls were. She describes her mother as "Frumpy Fran" because she wasn't into makeup or hairstyles or fashion at all; as a result Gail wasn't a girly girl either. But her biggest issue with her mother was that she was a "codependent doormat" for her dad. "He wiped his feet all over her, smacking her around and demanding his way all the time. My mom walked around in silent submission just to keep the peace. I thought that if this is what marriage is like, I don't want any part of it!"

In college Gail was assigned to a room with a girl named Candace, who seemed far more comfortable in her own feminine skin than Gail was. Gail just wished she could be as socially skilled as Candace, and she frequently looked to her for advice in matters of grooming and social interaction. Candace was also far more comfortable with her sexuality and decided to "help" Gail in that department, too, through lesbian experimentation. Though she knew this was wrong (this was a Bible college campus, by the way), the physical sensations of finally being accepted by someone were enough to make her press the Mute button on her conscience.

After several weeks Gail felt she must be in love. All of her hopes and dreams centered on being in Candace's presence. But Candace had started seeing a guy on campus she had high hopes might be "the one," so Candace started withdrawing sexually and emotionally from Gail. Eventually the relationship grew so tense that Candace asked to be reassigned to a different room. Gail was crushed and alone once again.

Unsure of her own sexual orientation, Gail also experimented with some guys on campus at group parties, where alcohol was involved, but those encounters were usually awkward and emotionally painful when the guys were willing to have sex with her but never willing to go out on a date with her. Feeling rejected by both genders, she simply didn't know which direction she "fit" best.

During grad school, Gail worked in the library and developed a girl crush on one of the other campus employees. The older woman responded positively for a while, but she then humiliated Gail with a public accusation of sexual harassment. It was at this point that Gail decided that she was through with relationships altogether. The prospect of ever being rejected again was enough to take all of the wind right out of her sexual sails.

That was when she attended the Exodus International Conference that I mentioned at the opening of this chapter. Through this new social circle she was able to form relationships with other like-minded individuals, both men and women, who were also seeking to become better stewards of their sexuality. She is also attending a church where she sees many marriages that appear very different from that of her parents, and she has hope that she can overcome the lure of lesbianism and find a man who will make a great life mate . . . and who can throw a ball as well as she can.

> "We all possess the power to hurt, but few the power to heal."
> —*from the song* "The Princess" *by Jim Bailey*

Recipe versus Relationship

As we read stories such as Monica's, Charlie's, and Gail's, we might try to identify the overcomer's "recipe" when we seek to answer the question "How do I find freedom?" If only there was a formula that could be followed!

But because we are wounded in relationship, our healing will also be found in relationship with others. Finding someone (a counselor, life coach, spiritual leader, spouse, or friend) you can be gut-level honest with about even the most confusing and embarrassing parts of your sexual struggles is a vital part of that process. As long as your struggle remains between your ears, it holds a lot more power over you. Verbalizing it with someone who will love you unconditionally and cheer you on to victory is an incredible growth experience.

To put some tools in your communication tool belt, let's explore some of the many possible reasons why same-sex relationships can seem so alluring.

MEN SEEKING MEN, WOMEN SEEKING WOMEN

If I had a dime for every woman who told me she was confused and bewildered by her own lesbian fantasies, I would be a very rich woman. This seems to be one of the most common struggles among Christian women today, especially with how glamorized lesbianism has become in our society. It has risen from gratuitous scenes in pornographic films to the mainstream media, with erotically positioned women appearing together on billboards, in magazines and movies, on television, and yes, all over the Internet.

With men, homosexuality is typically kept more on the "down low," but one doesn't have to look far to find a willing partner. In the words of one of my male friends, "Gay society welcomes you with such open arms. They make it so easy to fall down, and so hard to get back up!"

Whether in reality or fantasy, what is it that men are really looking for when they surf for gay porn, visit massage parlors or bathhouses, or seek a male lover? What is it that women are searching for as they watch girl-on-girl porn, visit a lesbian bar, or seek a female tryst?

First, let's look at a few possibilities that could be applicable to both men and women:

- *The "Rebel" Factor.* As we emotionally separate from our families of origin, we often reject our parents' spiritual and sexual values in an attempt to develop our own moral codes. If homosexuality was considered a big taboo, walking on that side of the street can satisfy one's urge to be shockingly rebellious.
- *The "Ghost" Principle.* Many men and women with same-sex fantasies have experienced a traumatic loss of a significant same-sex figure—through death, divorce, or emotional disconnection. Therefore, the homosexual fantasy is the brain's way of re-creating the male-male intimacy or the female-female intimacy that was lost in the mother-daughter or father-son relationship, or in the sister-sister or brother-brother relationship if the loss or disconnection was more with a sibling than with a parent.
- *The "Fix Me" Factor.* When one grows up with a dysfunctional parental relationship, it's easy to feel innately broken. The concept of having an older, wiser, same-sex partner who can "fix me" is the brain's way of trying to right that wrong, and it can make fantasizing about that particular person sexually appealing.
- *The "Cannibal" Effect.* As mentioned in chapter 5, cannibals make meals out of people whom they admire and want to emulate. Similarly, humans are usually attracted to someone who possesses a strength or characteristic that they believe they need more of in their own lives. Sometimes this desire for the *characteristic* is mistaken as sexual desire for the *person*.

A few further possibilities that could explain a man's pull toward other men are:

- *The "Aggression" Effect.* Because the male hormone testosterone contributes not just to sex drive but also to anger and aggression in men, many take out their anger (often toward emotionally absent fathers) in sexual ways toward other men.
- *The "Punish Me" Principle.* Because some men are subject to feeling an enormous amount of guilt and shame about their homosexual desires, they will often subject themselves to the pain and humiliation of being seduced or even raped by other men as some sort of punishment. This also creates a psychological absolution of their guilt if they were merely the "victims" of such sexual activities.
- *The "No Strings" Factor.* Men aren't wired to be as relational as women, and because gay sex often takes place in casual, anonymous group settings (such as bathhouses where aggressive group sex is common), the gay community provides a way for men to be sexual without relational commitment.

Finally, here are a few valid reasons why the female mind would view another woman's body as the object of her sexual fantasy:

- *The "Pinnacle" Principle.* It's interesting how God created the heavens and earth, then the animals, then man, then woman, then retired from creating anything else! The female body, which has inspired more music, art, and literature than anything else in this world, is surely the pinnacle of God's creation and, as such, is the object of many of our fantasies.

- *The "3-D" Effect.* Have you ever shopped for a greeting card and noticed that some just pop out from the racks because they are layered in a multidimensional manner? Or noticed how much more eye grabbing a 3-D movie is than a regular 2-D movie? Apply the same principle to the male and female bodies. The male body is beautiful, no doubt, but the curves of the female body definitely grab the eye of *all* human beings, not just men.
- *The "Safe Refuge" Effect.* When we fell and bumped our heads, made a bad grade, or had a fight with a friend, who did most of us run to? Mom. She was our safe refuge throughout most of life's storms. And because sex is a major form of comfort for us as adults, our minds may naturally gravitate in a female's direction when we seek the comfort of sexual arousal.
- *The "Familiarity" Factor.* Men are great providers and protectors, but women are usually the primary relators. Most of the face-to-face, eye-to-eye, voice-to-voice, skin-to-skin intimacy that we experience growing up is with our mothers, sisters, and female friends, and because human beings are drawn to the familiar, female intimacy is a rather natural comfort zone. In addition, a woman is more intimately familiar with the female body because that's the skin she's in, so same-sex fantasies may be a reflection of what she already knows, rather than what she wants more of.
- *The "Danger/Default" Factor.* When a woman is physically, sexually, or emotionally abused by a man, it's easy for her brain to conclude, *I'll never feel safe with any man.* By default, this sense of danger leaves only one gender in her mind with which she can be comfortable enough to explore her own sexuality—*women.*

Although these principles can help us make more sense out of same-sex attraction, we need to consider the bigger picture. Everything sexual looks rosy in our fantasies because that's the mental portrait we paint, but is the homosexual lifestyle really as rewarding as it may occasionally appear in our minds?

EXPOSING THE REALITY OF HOMOSEXUALITY

I asked several gay men and lesbian women to tell me what the homosexual lifestyle is *really* like—all of the glamour, mystery, and fantasy aside. In addition to the obvious fears of contracting HIV or other sexually transmitted infections, and of societal rejection, responses included the following:

- Fear of relational failure: few homosexual relationships ever make it past the two-year mark.[3]
- Fear of being cheated on: both gay men and lesbian women are often unfaithful to their lovers. Many self-described "monogamous" homosexual couples also reported an average of three to five partners in the past year.[4]
- Alcohol and drug abuse: many use not just illicit sex but also excessive drinking and drugs to medicate their emotional pain. Approximately 25 percent to 33 percent of people in the homosexual lifestyle are alcoholics, compared to 7 percent in the general population.[5]
- Domestic violence: because many homosexuals come from broken or abusive homes, anger and hostility easily translate into physical abuse. According to one study, women are forty-four times more likely to be abused by a lesbian lover than a husband, and men are three hundred times more likely to be abused in a homosexual relationship than in a heterosexual marriage.[6]

- A relentless pursuit of "the one": although a small percentage of homosexuals find a faithful lifetime partner, many will go through hundreds or even thousands of partners in search of relational satisfaction, which often seems elusive. One study reveals that 43 percent of white male homosexuals had sex with five hundred or more partners, with 28 percent having one thousand or more sex partners.[7]
- The "lesbian bed death" phenomenon: the intensity of lesbian relationships is typically very high in the beginning but dwindles quickly and can evolve to having little or *no* sexual intimacy between them at all.[8]
- Higher depression and suicide rates: studies indicate that lesbian, gay, bisexual, transgender, and questioning youth are up to four times more likely to attempt suicide than their heterosexual peers. And those who are rejected by their families are up to nine times more likely to attempt suicide than their heterosexual peers.[9]

In the article "Gay Rights: The Facts Behind Homosexuality," FaithFacts.org highlights the ravages of the lifestyle by examining these statistics and concluding that "homosexual behavior is marked by death, disease, disappointment, promiscuity, perversity, addiction, and misery."[10] Indeed, the social implications of choosing a gay lifestyle are minor compared to the physical, mental, and emotional torment one may face.

One of my coaching clients, Rick, who is now happily married to a wonderful woman, had identified himself for many years as gay. I asked Rick, "What led you into homosexuality?" His journey through childhood included an emotionally withdrawn father who was absent most of the time, early attempts at soothing his loneliness and isolation through masturbation, his mother's "don't do that" response, his pastor's "let me do that for you" molestation, his resulting confusion about all things sexual *and* spiritual, and drugs, alcohol, and suicide attempts during his teen and early adult years.

I asked Rick, "What led you out?" In his response, Rick recalled his days at Bible college. He would masturbate in the shower in the morning, then go to chapel. He'd peek at pornography and masturbate again during his lunch hour, then go for his prayer walk and beg God's forgiveness. Two hours later he'd be studying and feel the overwhelming urge to visit a male bathhouse on the outskirts of town. "I could have sex with five men that evening and still feel the need to masturbate myself to sleep!" he admitted. "The insatiability of it all was absolutely maddening! Sheer lust coursed through my veins most of the time, burning so strong that it could make me nauseous until I got a sexual release. I didn't *want* to do any of those things, but I felt as if I would never be able to concentrate on anything until I'd scratched that itch. So I kept scratching, which made the itch even worse. I realized that starving these desires was the only way I'd ever master them."

Fortunately Rick *did* master his desires. It has been more than fifteen years since he acted out sexually, and he says physical intimacy with another man is the *last* thing in the world he wants now. What are the *first* things he wants? To draw closer to his heavenly Father and to his earthly father, who has had a major life transformation; to be the best husband and dad to his wife and children; and to help other men recognize (and heal) the roots of their same-sex desires.

THE LURE OF BEING TRULY GAY

There has been much talk lately about how interesting the word *gay* is. The 1890s were called the "Gay Nineties," but one hundred years later, in 1990, that expression meant something entirely different. We've sung, "Don we now our *gay* apparel" in the Christmas song "Deck the Halls," and when we are with the Flintstones, we know "we'll have a *gay* old time!" But children now snicker at those lyrics.

The word *gay* used to mean "happy, merry, lively, cheerful, joyous, and jovial." Yet these words do *not* describe the gay lifestyle that so many have told me about. In fact, most homosexuals who feel certain that they were "born this way and can't help it" will also insist, "I would *never* choose this!" Their demeanor is often the antonym of *gay*—solemn, joyless, depressed, and melancholy.

Is there anything the church can do—anything *we* can do—to expose the deeper meaning behind homosexual thoughts in the minds of those who romanticize and fantasize about being *gay*? Rather than point an accusatory finger at them, perhaps we can point them to God, who is the source of *true* happiness, merriment, joy, and gaiety.

Roxane Hill, a participant in my B.L.A.S.T. mentorship group for aspiring writers and speakers, recently gave a speech in which she shared a story she heard on the radio about a medical team during wartime. The team's responsibility was to go from hospital bed to hospital bed and label patients' files with either "medical hope" or "no medical hope."

As they reviewed one man's chart and labeled him "no medical hope," the patient responded, "*No*, my name is *John*." One of the nurses later went back and changed John's label, scratching out the *no* and changing his status to "medical hope."

We must do the same thing. We can no longer look at people identified by homosexuality or dealing with same-sex attractions, shake our heads, and declare, "There's no hope for them." Like John, these individuals have names, faces, and often painful life experiences and, like all of us, aren't beyond God's ability to restore, heal, and transform.

Rather than allow our brothers and sisters to grapple with their gay and lesbian fantasies alone, in shame and secrecy, let's give them hope. Let's be safe sounding boards. Let's help them expose the deeper meanings behind their sexual thoughts and show them in both word and deed that the body of Christ *does* care for them . . . that *we* care for them.

BEHIND THE CURTAIN: TRACING THE ROOTS OF SAME-SEX FANTASIES

When I asked for testimonies from people who struggled with same-sex attraction, I was inundated with responses—enough to write a completely separate book. Poring over each one of them carefully, I decided that these two had to be shared.

When Mama Ain't Happy . . .

William (age twenty-seven) writes:

> After taking a college psychology class, I suspected that my adoptive mother never bonded with me in the way that she did with her biological children. I always felt like the "odd man out" in our house.
>
> My dad worked a lot, and my mom seemed to be stressed all the time and took that stress out on me. I was the oldest, so I had to work hard to help her manage, but there was no pleasing her, no measuring up to her standards of perfection. I couldn't make my bed right. I couldn't fold the laundry right. I felt like a total screwup. I really did try, but I learned early in life that there was no pleasing a woman, at least not my mom. And because I could never please her, I was always being physically punished or verbally berated.

My dad, however, felt the need to compensate for my mother's coldness and brutality. He was incredibly patient and kind, and would sometimes crawl into my bed to tuck me in. I knew that he loved me and felt my pain, and I felt really safe as long as he was home to protect me.

The thing that's been most bewildering to me as a teenager and young adult is my fantasies of having a gay lover. Although I've struggled for many years with looking at guy-on-guy pornography on occasion, I've not physically acted out on this overwhelming desire. Fortunately, I've just never had the opportunity and have managed to avoid places like gay massage parlors where I knew I could find relief with some sort of random encounter. Even if I was willing to "go there," I'd want a real relationship, not a one-night stand. I don't think I was born with this desire. I think it was cultivated in me throughout a very long and painful childhood.

My biggest fear is that these fantasies will never go away . . . or that I might act out on them someday and live to regret it. I'm just grateful that I know God well enough to be assured that He'd love me just the same, even if I were to choose this path. He understands my pain more than I do. My other fear is that if I get married to a woman, she'll either discover my dark secret or turn out to be just as cold and callous as my mom. I don't think I could survive that.

For the parents who are reading this, I don't want dads to think that they shouldn't be affectionate toward their sons. They definitely should be. But mothers need to be sensitive to how much boys want to be a hero to the women in their lives, even to their moms. When we feel like zeros instead of heroes in a mom's eyes, we easily calculate that women simply aren't a soft place to land.

However, there are many women who, because of unique family dynamics, consider women a *very* soft place to land. Cindy is one of those women.

Cindy's Search for a Soft Place to Land

Cindy (age thirty-one, married with one child) writes:

> I was nineteen when I walked into a friend's living room and saw her older brother watching porn on their big-screen television. What I recall most about that incredibly awkward moment was that the porn stars were both female, and they were having sex with each other, which was something I didn't even know women could do.
>
> Unable to get that scene out of my mind, I sought out similar scenarios on the Internet, masturbating to those images and being astounded at the intensity of my orgasm. I began to wonder if I could be a lesbian because it was overwhelmingly more pleasurable to envision being intimate with another woman than it was with a man.
>
> I never told anyone about this experience, and within a few years I was married to a great guy and we had a beautiful baby girl. We were attending a church where the women's ministry leader, Lydia, was this really beautiful woman—inside and out—and she was great to take me under her wing. She was maybe twelve years older than me, and she seemed very open to discussing anything that was on my mind, so I told her about my earlier experiences. I also confessed to her that in order to reach orgasm with my husband, I usually entertained lesbian fantasies in my head.
>
> In hindsight, there may have been a small part of me that hoped she would identify with this issue and provide a safe

relationship where I could "explore" whether I was really a lesbian or not. After all, that's what I'd been encouraged to do by the media, especially *The Oprah Show,* which frequently featured adult women or men finally "coming out of the closet" to "own their homosexuality."

Fortunately, Lydia was more trustworthy than that and didn't take advantage of my vulnerability at all. She just assured me that sexual confusion is relatively normal and asked a series of questions over the course of several meetings together to try to help me make sense of it all. We discussed my relationships with my mom, dad, and siblings. I told her about how my father was very emotionally distant and verbally abusive to everyone in the house if he was having a bad day. On a few occasions, he flew off the handle and hit one of us but would always break down and cry afterward, begging our forgiveness. We just learned to walk on eggshells around him while my mother made excuses for his behavior and assured us that he really did love us but didn't always know how to show it.

My mom was very attentive and adored her children, and I loved her deeply. I still do. But in 1995, she changed—we all changed—when the world as we'd always known it came crashing down around us.

I was fourteen, and my younger sister, Penny, was ten. Penny was spending the night with some close friends. Their house caught fire in the middle of the night when lightning struck their roof. Everyone inside was burned to death, including my sister.

We all tried to cope as best we could, but my mother was never the same fun-loving, affectionate person. She was more like a walking zombie, staring into space while putting one foot in front of the other, assuring everyone she was fine, but completely oblivious to the needs of anyone else around her.

As I shared these stories with Lydia, it became crystal clear why lesbian fantasies would invade my mind on occasion. She explained that when we're experiencing orgasm, our brain has a way of "righting all wrongs," or "soothing our pain." We orchestrate events in our imagination to line up with what our soul longs for most, and I've spent years longing for my little sister to have survived that fire, and longing for my mother to snap out of her grief and return to being the woman that I felt so safe with and cherished by.

In light of these connections, I've never again questioned my sexual orientation. I'm a heterosexual woman who has a great husband and a great sex life, and even if lesbian fantasies creep in on occasion to distract me from the pain I'll always carry around in my heart, that's okay. I control them. They do not control me.

We are the captains of our sexuality ships. We may not always have control over what thoughts initially come into our minds when we are sexually aroused or understand why they include certain scenarios, but we have complete control over how much energy we want to give them. We decide which ones we pay attention to and which ones get ignored. We determine which direction to take at every turn, and with God's help, we have the power to stay completely on course as we navigate the waters of healthy sexuality.

8

Our Fascination with Pleasure, Pain, and Power

Growing up without a plethora of money meant we made toys out of whatever we could find. We couldn't afford a drum set, nor did we have a place for one, but we had pots, pans, and wooden spoons that allowed us the same thrill in the middle of the kitchen floor. A swimming pool was always on our birthday wish list, along with the proverbial pony for Christmas, but alas, those things were never in the budget. We made do just fine, however, with a garden sprinkler and a border collie instead.

But the most creative use of our recreational energies was when we played outside with absolutely nothing except the sun and our bodies. The neighborhood kids would get together and stage shadow plays or shadow dances. Standing in the middle of the oil-topped road on a sunny day, our bodies would cast long, dark shadows across the pavement, and with the right posture and arm movements, we could become anything we wanted to be.

In order to witness the play or dance as it unfolded, however, we couldn't have our faces toward the sun. If we did, all of the action took place behind our backs, out of our lines of sight. To critique our own performance and determine what the others were doing, we had to turn around and face our shadows.

Consider this chapter our way of facing our shadows as we explore the darker side of our sexuality, looking specifically at rape and incest fantasies, domination and submission, and sadomasochism, and what these mental movies really mean to us as human beings.

These topics haven't been discussed much in Christian circles, so this might feel a little scary, but it's not nearly as scary as turning our backs and remaining oblivious to the deeper meaning behind these common sexual thoughts.

"DON'T! . . . STOP! . . . DON'T STOP!"

Even though actually being raped is considered one of the most traumatic and psychologically disturbing things one could experience, there's obviously something about the fantasy alone that floats some people's boat. And fiction authors are obviously aware of this, as lead female characters experience rape in approximately 54 percent of romance novels.[1] So why would we fantasize or dream about something that we'd *never* want to actually experience?

Returning to our original theory of sexual fantasies being the brain's way of trying to heal itself from some trauma, we must ask, "What kind of life experience might someone have had that would require such a forceful scenario to open up the brain's pathways toward pleasure?"

In a rape scene the victim has absolutely no choice about whether sex is going to take place or not. It is being forced upon the victim. And solely in the fantasy, this feels like a *good* thing. Perhaps that is because the fantasizer is a very passive person, and the idea of someone dominating and making sexual decisions for him or her is appealing. Or maybe it's so the victim doesn't have to take any responsibility for what's happening. The victim doesn't have to feel guilty about being "loose" or promiscuous. These fears of feeling responsible, guilty, or promiscuous very possibly stem from having repressed sexuality, which often happens when a person is raised in well-meaning Christian homes with the mind-set of, "Sex is dirty and shameful, and those who engage in it willingly are dirty and shameful too."

Guilt and shame aren't compatible with an orgasmic mind-set, so the rape fantasy takes all guilt and shame off the table, making room for a feast of pleasure, even if being raped is something that would *not* be pleasurable in real life at all. It's quite fascinating how the mind works to ensure our sexual fulfillment, not because we're perverts or horrible people, but simply because we're designed by God as sexual beings to the core.

Of course, in the rape fantasy the fantasizer isn't always the victim. Sometimes the fantasizer is the perpetrator—probably because he or she must compartmentalize past negative emotions that aren't compatible with becoming sexually aroused. Dr. Michael J. Bader, author of *Arousal: The Secret Logic of Sexual Fantasies*, explains the deeper meaning behind this fantasy in the perpetrator's mind:

> By turning the psychological tables, by being the one who is violently frightening and violating rather than frightened and violated, such a man can feel momentarily relieved of this obstacle and feel safe enough to get aroused.[2]

So most likely the person who fantasizes about raping someone has felt an extremely scary sense of helplessness in the past, and this fantasy is the person's way of compensating for such trauma. Bader gives further insight into the difference between someone who fantasizes that he brings a woman pleasure by raping her versus someone who rapes without regard to the victim's pleasure at all:

> A man who enjoys a woman's actual pain without any fantasy that the woman is secretly enjoying it is likely a man who has somehow been, in his most intimate relationships growing up, victimized, humiliated, or wounded.[3]

This confirms the theory that "hurting people hurt people." Prisons are filled with individuals who've been hurt so badly they don't know what else to do but repeat the pattern. Many are culturally conditioned, either through real-world experiences or through the fantasy world of pornography, to equate sex with violence, and vice versa.

We can't always assume that men are the only ones with such violent fantasies. I met an incredibly sweet woman (I'll call her Sarah) years ago at a conference for sexual healing. She was there primarily to deal with her fantasies of raping men. While on a walk together, she offered a glimpse into the past that drove her in this mental direction.

One day a man posing as a pest control agent knocked on her apartment door, saying that he was there to spray for ants. Sarah let him in, and within seconds he had the hose of his spray gun wrapped around her throat. He forced her to the floor, raped her, slit her throat with a knife, and left her for dead. Fortunately Sarah did not die but spent many months in physical and mental rehabilitation.

A year later Sarah's friends insisted that getting out more often would cheer her up, so they would go to dance clubs and parties. Sarah found herself gravitating toward certain men, striking up a conversation, having a drink or two, then letting a man take her to his place. Rather than continuing the conversation and getting to know one another, Sarah would immediately "go for the kill," forcing herself onto him sexually.

Sarah reflected, "Some men might not have minded, but I never took time to find out. It wasn't about *them* and what they wanted. It was about *me* and what I wanted. It wasn't as much about the sex as the fact that I needed to be in complete control from the very beginning. I needed to 're-create the scenario' in order to 'win this time.' I realize now it was nothing short of rape."

Had Sarah been honest about her rape fantasies with a counselor, perhaps she could have made sense out of them before dragging other people (innocent victims) into her situation. If she only had taken the time to recognize her overwhelming need to regain her personal power as something that could be positive rather than negative, she could have opted for choices that would have brought healing rather than hopelessness. For example, she could have started a support group for similar victims or begun ministering to women at homeless shelters, where there are many who have been sexually abused, or volunteered as a telephone counselor with a rape hotline. Robert Johnson supports the notion that we can harness the power of our fantasies and sublimate them into incredibly productive pursuits:

> Because we often repress the best parts of ourselves and think of them as "negative" qualities, some of the richest parts of the self—even the voice of God itself—can only partake in our lives by "stealing" our time, stealing our energy through compulsions and neurosis, and slipping into our lives in the unprotected places where our guard is down [such as in dreams and fantasies]. . . .
>
> Our egos divide the world into positive and negative, good and bad. Most aspects of our shadows, these qualities that we see as "negative," would in fact be valuable strengths if

> we made them conscious. Characteristics that look immoral, barbaric, or embarrassing to us are the negative side of a valuable energy, a capacity that we could make use of. You will never find anything in the unconscious that will not be useful when it is made conscious and brought to the right level.[4]

Consciousness. Awareness. This is exactly what I hope this book brings. It's only through this avenue that we find the deep, inner healing we crave. We can't take captive a thought that we are not aware of, refuse to acknowledge, or minimize its power. We can take thoughts captive only as we become painfully aware of them. That awareness (coupled with submission to the power made available to us through Christ) makes us much safer people to be around.

Unfortunately, some of us have been around people, even within our own family, who proved to be not-so-safe to be around . . .

WHEN THE MIND SAYS, INCEST IS BEST

Just like the other sexual distortions we have discussed so far, incest dates all the way back to the book of Genesis, when Lot's daughters got their father drunk and had sex with him. Unfortunately incestuous desires didn't stop there.

For our first coaching session, I met Mandy at a Starbucks in Dallas. After about an hour she happened to notice a man sitting in the corner, staring straight at her while he ate a banana. The conversation came to a pause, and Mandy excused herself to the restroom and was gone for quite some time. I knocked to see if she was okay. She opened the door but was standing at the sink, looking deathly pale, and holding her stomach as if she needed to vomit.

After several minutes she regained her composure enough to return to our table. I asked if she wanted to talk about what had just occurred, and she complied, saying, "Any time I see someone eating a banana, it gives me flashbacks to when I was ten or so, when my grandfather forced me to perform oral sex on him." Mandy went on to explain that oral sex was something that she could receive but not perform for her husband because of all the negative emotions it triggered.

"It makes me want to gag," she continued. "But if I told you what goes through my head as I'm receiving oral sex, *you* would gag!" I challenged her to try me, but only if she was ready to share that information. She knew I was doing research for this book, so she was eager to see if I could help her make sense of it all.

"I've always been angry at my grandfather for doing what he did, but that was a one-time thing. I've been even angrier at my father for what he did over and over."

"Did he abuse you sexually as well?" I asked.

"No, quite the opposite," she replied with tears weighing heavily against her lower eyelids. "He ignored me my whole life. He was a single dad, and he traveled on business, so that's why I stayed with my grandparents a lot. I longed for him to want to spend time with me, to find me interesting, to think I was beautiful. So the way I most often experience orgasm is to envision my own father showing a sexual interest in me. I've often thought, *Why couldn't it have been Dad instead of Granddad who wanted me?*" Crinkling her nose with disgust, she asked, "Isn't that absolutely *horrible?*"

A few years ago, out of ignorance, I may have concurred and fueled her fears that this was a sick and twisted fantasy. But in light of all I've learned, I could see how the fantasy would make perfect sense in her mind; it was merely her brain's way of trying to heal itself from feelings of rejection and emotional neglect from the most important person in her life. The fact that her dad had no time or attention to give her was horrible. The fact that her grandfather sexually abused her was horrible. But *she* was not a horrible person for trying to heal those sexual and emotional scars the only way her brain knew how.

Of course, sometimes an incest fantasy doesn't originate in the child's mind toward a parent. Sometimes it's a parent who fantasizes about being with a son or daughter, or a surrogate son or daughter figure. I recall watching one of the first episodes of *Desperate Housewives* to see what all of the controversy was about. I was angered by a scene where Eva Longoria seduces a teenage boy in his own bedroom decorated with sports pennants and soccer trophies. As she is mounting him on his bed, she reaches toward his nightstand. She grabs a picture frame containing a photo of the boy in his Little League uniform, as if she's trying to erase the reminder that he's still a child.

What could possibly be operating in the mind of an adult who wants to have sex with someone young enough to be his or her own child? Let's turn to yet another of Dr. Bader's insightful theories about why women might be tempted to pursue a son figure and why men might fantasize about a daughter figure:

> The son—inexperienced, full of hormonal pressures, and under the sway of the mother's authority—reassures the mother against fears of rejection. The son is enthralled and seduced by the mother's womanly sexuality and isn't in a position to be "choosy." On the other hand, the son's youth conveys a sexual vitality and inexhaustible carnal desire that counteracts the woman's worries and guilt about draining a man her own age. The boy is full of sexual vigor, and as a result, she is too.
>
> Similarly, fathers' incest fantasies about their daughters or daughter-figures also carry mixed meanings. The girls are nubile and inexperienced, open to whatever the father, or father

> figure, can teach them. The men are therefore unconsciously reassured against the dangers of failure, of disappointing their partners in the same way that they might feel with their wives or that they might have felt with their mothers.[5]

In other words, fear of losing our own sex appeal and energies as we grow older is primarily what might fuel such a fantasy. But of course, we don't need to turn the fantasy into any sort of reality, dragging another human beings into our stuff for a personal ego stroke at *their* expense. As Christians, and as humans, we have a responsibility to be good stewards of our sexuality and bring harm to no one. The more we understand the human psyche and how it might operate in various seasons of our lives, from cradle to grave, the safer everyone else will be in our presence.

> **"Each of us must turn inward and destroy in himself all that he thinks he ought to destroy in others."[6]**
> *—Etty Hillesum*

The final dark side we will face in this chapter is a term that has been thrust into the mainstream by the popular Fifty Shades trilogy—BDSM—which stands for bondage, domination, sadism, and masochism.

HURTS SO GOOD . . . OR DOES IT?

At first glance the fact that someone would get a kick out of tying up or inflicting pain or humiliating someone sexually is unimaginable. Yet many imagine, quite vividly! According to Brett Kahr's *Who's Been Sleeping in Your Head?* study:

- 25 percent of respondents fantasize about being tied up.
- 18 percent of men and 7 percent of women fantasize about spanking someone.

- 11 percent of men and 13 percent of women fantasize about being spanked.[7]

Speaking of being tied up and spanked, many people have asked, "What do you think of *Fifty Shades of Grey*?" I admit that I have all kinds of mixed emotions.

When it comes to lead character (and sadist) Christian Grey, age twenty-six, I've wanted to slap him into next week for inflicting women with intense pain and degradation. In the story, when we learn of his "Red Room of Pain," he has already abused fifteen women with his bizarre sadomasochistic fantasies. The other part of me says, at least he's acutely aware of his fetish, is seeing a counselor, and is up-front and honest about his desires and expectations, even going to the trouble of spelling it all out through a "domination/submission" contract that he asks women to sign beforehand.

Regarding the heroine of the story, Anastasia Steele, age twenty-one, part of me wants to cheer for her courage in exploring her own sexuality, but *only* if this could have been done *within the context of marriage*, not a dating relationship—and especially not with a man she met little more than five minutes ago! I wanted to shake her by the shoulders and tell her, "Wake up, baby doll! Don't give a guy your virginity, thinking, *There's lots of things I really don't like or trust about this guy, but he's so sexy and rich that I'll risk it! Surely my love will change him!*" It may work that way in novels and in fantasy, but not in real life.

However, when people ask what I think of the novel, they aren't always interested in a literary criticism or an opinion of the characters' morals or choices. Sometimes what they're really asking is, "What do you think about BDSM?"

Again, mixed emotions. The legalist inside of me (most of us have one in there somewhere) wants to throw a stone and say, that's *bad*! Under *any* circumstance! No one should *ever* do that! But then I remember how God is teaching me to read between the lions and avoid all extremes in either a legalistic or a liberal direction. So I slow down long enough to consider the fact that there are happily married Christian couples who, for deep psychological reasons, *both* find pleasure in BDSM activities. What are we to make of that?

Perhaps she likes playing the dominatrix role while he enjoys submitting to her control. Or she likes to role-play being passive and obedient, while her husband pursues her with raw aggression. What's behind this type of fantasy?

If you think in opposite terms, you discover possible clues. For people who want to dominate and control, they most likely felt out of control and dominated by a significant person in their past. By being the one in charge (the "master") for a change, they regain a lost sense of power. For people who prefer the submissive role (the "slave"), they most likely enjoy relinquishing control so they don't have to fear holding the hot potato of responsibility, guilt, worry, or anxiety. "I was forced to do it" is the scapegoat that provides permission to enjoy sexual pleasure.

From a physical perspective, one might wonder how infusing sexual activities with pain could possibly be pleasurable. Scientists have actually discovered that the area of the brain associated with pain is stimulated in women especially during sexual arousal, so there is actually a distinct connection between pain and pleasure.[8] This may explain why some (although certainly not all) women like being spanked during sexual activity.

From a psychological perspective it is not difficult to see how someone who has experienced verbal, emotional, physical, or sexual abuse in the past could naturally gravitate in the direction of domination/submission role-play. In this fantasy the victim becomes a victor. The better their sense of power and control, the better climax they experience.

Dr. Bader provides further insight as to why BDSM "works" for abuse victims:

> One essential aspect of a sexually masochistic fantasy is that the pain and helplessness are voluntarily created and experienced. The helplessness is not real. The masochist is always in control of the type, duration, and degree of pain that she or he endures. The adult indulging in a fantasy of sexual surrender or abasement is actually saying to her or himself: "I'm recreating a terrifying and traumatic scene, but this time I'm in control because I'm scripting the scene as much as my partner is." The "victim" in the adult sadomasochistic scenario is not really a victim. She or he is constructing a situation in which the pathogenic beliefs that stemmed from childhood abuse are being momentarily disproved, thereby creating the conditions of safety necessary to become aroused. Trauma is turned on its head. The slave turns out to be the master, and the master is sexually dependent on the slave. A game is set up in which the victim of childhood abuse finally gets to win.[9]

We don't always get to choose what fantasies work for us on our journey toward sexual arousal and fulfillment. There are many who absolutely hate the fact that this type of fantasy is such a turn-on for them. I hope that understanding the psychological underpinnings of the scenario will help to absolve these individuals of false guilt and inspire them to treat this fantasy with kid gloves so as not to bring any unnecessary harm to their partners. The reality is that even if one spouse is into BDSM, that's no guarantee that the other will be on board, especially if safe boundary lines aren't strictly adhered to. When people get hurt for *real*, the whole scenario goes awry, and the sense of trust and safety required to experience sexual pleasure completely disappears. Just ask Terra, who e-mailed the following letter when she learned I was writing this book:

> I've been hearing all of the hoopla about *Fifty Shades of Grey*, and I'm shocked and scared for many who are reading those books and most likely concluding that this is what women want. It honestly makes my stomach flip-flop because I just divorced a man very similar to the lead character, Christian Grey. (I'll call him "Gary.")
>
> Before I started dating Gary I had promised myself that I would spend the rest of my life with the person I gave my virginity to. But because of the home I was raised in, "technical virginity" seemed to be the best I could do. My parents had a very open and explicit sex life. They didn't bother hiding their pornography, sex toys, and bisexuality from us kids. My dad also had a pedophilia problem, making sexual advances toward me when I was twelve. Fortunately, I was able to thwart those advances, but of course, they left deep scars.
>
> When Gary and I started seeing each other, I gave myself to him sexually—virginity and all—within the first two weeks of dating. I was nineteen at the time, very lonely and tired of abstaining from intercourse. Only afterward did I find out what some of his sexual interests included. Wrist cuffs, dog collars, and rope bondage . . . gagging and blindfolding . . . anal sex . . . cross-dressing . . . spreader bars for restraining purposes . . . "torture porn" where women are tied up and beaten senseless . . . choking his partner to "heighten" sexual climaxes. These last two scared me the most. He'd want me to watch torture porn with him so I could be the outlet for his sexual jollies, but I'd just sit there mortified that any

human being could watch that and be okay with it. And I couldn't help but wonder if he was ever going to beat me that severely. He would just laugh and tell me to lighten up when I expressed my grave concern.

He joined some gothic Web communities with other people who were into that sort of stuff. He'd learn new things from them and then want to try it with me. I wondered if *any* extreme would ever satisfy him. It seemed things always had to be a little more unusual, painful, or dangerous than the last time. I finally drew the line when he wanted to put a cell phone inside of me. He was aroused by the idea that he could tease me sexually in public by dialing the number and having it vibrate. I realized then that I was just a toy in his twisted sexual toy box.

The majority of my relationship with him, I felt hollow and insufficient. I was always aware that "me and only me" in our bedroom would never be enough. That would be too boring for him. I felt I was never pretty enough or exotic enough. I lost my self-esteem and my own desires in order to become the little plaything he wanted me to be.

You may be horrified to hear these things about a "Christian" couple, or perhaps you've heard even worse things. People that I've shared this secret with have asked, "Why in the world did you stay?"

I felt like I was trapped. I tried leaving the relationship before we got married, but couldn't move past the promise I'd made since I'd already given him my virginity. Once we were married, I felt like I was going against God if I divorced. So all that I did with him was out of a sense of obligation to be a dutiful partner and wife, not because I wanted to do those things myself.

I've had to go through a lot of therapy to be able to recognize what parts of our sex life were just way too much for me, when I should have said no, and why I didn't stand my ground at the time. I was very immature and incredibly codependent, having no will of my own other than to please him.

I do realize now that I should never have married Gary in the first place. I didn't learn until after I'd walked the aisle that just because you have sex with someone before marriage doesn't mean you have to stay with them, especially when *big red flags* begin flapping in the breeze! I've come to believe that, yes, God sees premarital sex as sin, but two wrongs—having sex *and* getting married to try to fix it—don't make a right. I'm just thankful that God sees all of our mistakes and freely forgives us when we repent, run from repeating those mistakes, and seek refuge in Him.

Fortunately, I'm now married to a man who treats me with respect and loves me like Christ loved the church. He'd never ask me to do anything degrading or painful. I can't believe the stark contrast between these two men—literally, like night and day—and how I have felt in relationship with each of them. I'm so thankful that I found the courage to go through with divorcing my first husband because I just don't believe women should have to succumb to such degradation and pain for the sake of love, commitment, or even marriage. I can't fathom that what Gary insisted on doing to me was okay with God.[10]

God's plan for our sexual pleasure does *not* include doing things that cause others pain. If you are in a relationship where a fun fantasy evolves into a painful reality, jump ship! No one deserves to be sexually abused—not as a child or as an adult.

I have to take advantage of the opportunity presented here to speak out about sadistic pornography. My goal isn't to shock or offend, so let me remind you that this has been a societal issue since Judges 19, when the Levite's concubine was gang-raped, tortured by evil men in the village, then cut up by her master into twelve pieces to be sent to the twelve tribes of Israel. Amazing how some things never change in a society of sinners.

We assume the reason a man wants to look at porn is that he loves women and loves sex. But when it comes to "torture porn," nothing could be further from the truth. Voyeurs of such sadistic scenarios don't *love* women and sex. They *hate* women, fear sexual intimacy, and therefore seek revenge on all women because some from their past have made them feel rejected and impotent. In *Empire of Illusion*, Chris Hedges states:

> Porn has become so embedded and accepted in the culture, especially among the young, that sexual humiliation, abuse, rape, and physical violence have emerged into a socially acceptable expression. . . . Absolute power over others almost always expresses itself through sexual sadism. . . .
>
> [Porn] today focuses less on sex between a man and a woman and increasingly on groups of men beating off on a woman's face or tearing her anus open with their penises. Porn has evolved to its logical conclusion. It first turned women into sexual commodities and then killed women as human beings. And it has won the culture war. Pornography and the commercial mainstream have fused. . . . [Porn] extinguishes the sacred and the human to worship power, control, force, and pain. It replaces empathy, eros, and compassion with the illusion that we are gods.[11]

I believe Hedges hit the nail on the head with that last statement. As humans we can become obsessed with obtaining power, but only God possesses ultimate power. The best we can ever hope to do is to stay as intimately connected as possible to our almighty God so we can access His unlimited power to *control* our own sexual drives and to be a blessing rather than a burden to those we encounter throughout our lifetimes.

THE LIFE-GIVING UNION OF DARK AND LIGHT

As we hear stories of men sexually torturing women, priests sexually abusing altar boys, teachers seducing students, spouses cheating on one another, and parents molesting their own children, our hearts break for the victims and for our sexually broken culture. These are merely examples of people being bit by their own fantasies because they were too afraid to turn around and face them. They weren't mature enough to sift through their own shadows and make sense of the darkness that dwells there, so they focused on the fruit of their fantasies rather than the roots.

Robert Bly writes in *A Little Book on the Human Shadow*, "Plants are asleep, and so they live always in the dark side, though their leaves reach out for the light. So we could say that each weed in our back yard unites dark and light."[12] It's a simple analogy, but the wisdom runs deep.

What we see as a flower or tree or any other kind of plant is just an extension of what's at the root. You won't see magnolia leaves sprouting from the roots of a dogwood tree, nor will you see ears of corn shoot off a cucumber vine. What we are in the light is determined by who we are in the dark. Our fruit is merely the product of our roots.

Only through tending to our mental, emotional, and spiritual roots will we bear the healthiest fruit possible. Ignore the roots, and the plant will suffer. Nurture the roots, and the plant will thrive.

BEHIND THE CURTAIN: WHAT'S UP WITH SEXUAL FETISHES?

A sexual fetish occurs when someone bonds with an *object* rather than a person (usually early in life), sexualizing that object and deriving intense pleasure from it either while alone or with a partner. I have heard of fetishes ranging from panties to ponytails, lipstick to leather, and high heels to handcuffs.

Being turned on by a certain "thing" may sound sick and twisted to some people, but others completely get it even though they may not necessarily understand *why* they experience a sexual penchant for some particular item. I would like to introduce you to a couple of people who recently learned the *why* behind their fetishes, starting with Stan.

Stan's Stocking Fetish

I first met Stan and Doris when they approached me for marriage coaching. Their presenting issue was that Doris was unresponsive to Stan's sexual advances. "She just lies there like a limp fish," Stan complained.

"I'm not just lying there, Stan. I'm lying there fuming!" Doris retorted in his direction. Looking at me with one eyebrow cocked, she added, "You can cut the tension in our bedroom with a knife!"

"Can you tell me about the source of the tension?" I inquired.

"My wife has cut me off sexually! That's the source of the tension!" Stan insisted.

This wasn't my first marriage-coaching rodeo, so I knew there had to be more to the story. "Would you say that you've 'cut him off sexually' as Stan describes, Doris?"

"I guess looking at our most recent sexual history, that would be true," she stated matter-of-factly. "But, Stan, why don't you tell her the reason that I've cut you off."

Stan shot Doris a look that could kill, as if to say, "There's no need to go there!" But the can of worms had been opened. Looking down at his folded hands in his lap like a little boy who'd been caught with his hand in the cookie jar, Stan managed to cough up the words: "I crossed a line."

Through several rounds of questions I learned that when they married three years earlier, Stan disclosed that he had a pantyhose fetish. The sight, smell, and feel of well-worn stockings served as an intense aphrodisiac. He would caress them while making love to his wife, or he would use them in a masturbatory fashion when alone, especially while traveling. While Doris didn't understand what the big turn-on was for Stan about dirty pantyhose, she was willing to live with it. "My first husband's fetish turned out to be child pornography, so this seemed incredibly tame in comparison!" she explained.

However, Doris had made a painful discovery. While traveling on business, Stan had sent text messages to two coworkers traveling with him, asking if he could swing by their hotel room door to retrieve the pantyhose they'd worn to dinner that evening. "He even offered them a new pair in exchange, which told me that this was very premeditated on his part. For him to pack unopened pantyhose for a business trip is very telling about his intentions, don't you think?" she begged, right eyebrow raised again.

Stan sat in his chair, shoulders slumped, looking like he just dropped his ice-cream cone in the dirt. I asked Stan, "Do you have any idea how you developed this particular fetish?" He shook his head from side to side without making eye contact. I asked, "Would you like to explore it together so that, perhaps, we can make some sense of it?"

His head rose slowly but inquisitively. "How can you make any sense whatsoever out of the fact that I'm a *freak*?" he argued.

Assuring him that he was no more a freak than any other sexual human being, we agreed to spend the next session trying to connect the current fruit of his fantasy to some childhood roots.

At our next session I learned that as a boy Stan spent many of his free afternoons at his grandmother's house. As he recalled memories of his grandmother and their time together, Stan remembered that he'd often play at her feet while she sat reading or watching television in her recliner. "She'd always have pantyhose on, and I enjoyed how her nylons felt on my fingertips, so I'd rub her feet often. She would smile and moan about how good it felt—not in a sexual way, but in an appreciative way, and it made me feel like she valued me and liked having me around.

"I can remember one time that I wanted to rub her feet, but she was still in her robe and slippers, so she didn't have pantyhose on. Instead of rubbing her bare feet, I went into her room, opened her dresser drawers, and found a pair, asking her to put them on. She laughed and obliged."

Stan also remembered how his grandmother would occasionally cross her legs and perch him atop her ankle, bouncing him up and down pony-ride–style while he straddled her pantyhose-clad leg. "She didn't know that it felt really good to me and that I was really humping her leg when I hopped on asking for one of her pony rides," he acknowledged.

I asked if these memories gave him any insights as to why women's pantyhose would cause the sexual parts of his brain to light up like a Christmas tree. "I haven't thought about all of that in decades," he exclaimed, "and I don't know that I'd ever have made the connection without dissecting it like this!"

"Stan," I responded, "it's one thing to find yourself sexually aroused by an inanimate object. Doris doesn't seem to have a problem with that. But can you understand how she would have a problem with you soliciting dirty pantyhose from other women?" I then asked if he'd ever crossed that line before this recent incident.

Stan remembered that when he was around ten years old, an older woman was staying overnight in their home. He couldn't help but notice that she was wearing pantyhose and was intrigued. So intrigued, in fact, that he entered her room the next day to see if those dirty pantyhose might be found. Retrieving them from her suitcase, he dropped his shorts and rubbed the hose against his crotch to try to re-create that familiar old feeling. To his surprise, the woman walked into the room, catching him in the act. But rather than respond with shock and horror, the woman smiled and assured Stan, "It's okay. Your secret is safe with me. In fact, you can just keep those if you'd like."

We discussed how being gifted with a pair of dirty pantyhose when you are ten years old is very different from asking a woman for her dirty hose as an adult, especially a married adult. "If the scenario were different—if your wife were approaching another man, asking him for something sexually arousing rather than coming to you—wouldn't you feel threatened? Even cheated on, perhaps?" He acknowledged the truth of that statement.

We also discussed the inherent dangers of asking women for such an intimate item. How a job (and paycheck) could be lost. How his reputation could be damaged and his credibility shot down. But most of all, he didn't want to lose Doris. He loved her enough to acknowledge his sin and beg her forgiveness, assuring her it would never happen again. And she could take as long as she needed to warm back up to him sexually, as it would require time to reestablish trust and intimacy.

In light of the clearer boundary lines established, Doris was merciful and extended absolution. "I love you too," she replied, "pantyhose fetish and all."

Laura's Dirty Little Secret

After speaking on the topic of controlling our sexual fantasies before they control us, I was approached by a college-age woman with a look of sheer terror on her face. Although in her early twenties, Laura looked almost twice that age. It was obvious that life had been hard for Laura, and she wore the evidence all over her face and slumped shoulders. She waited until the crowd thinned enough that she wouldn't be overheard, then asked if she could have two minutes of my time. I offered ten if she needed it.

"I have a sexual fantasy that I promise you've never heard of," she began.

I grinned and assured her that after many years of speaking, writing, and counseling on the subject of healthy sexuality, there wasn't much I hadn't already heard. "Why don't you try me?" I suggested.

Eyes downcast, she spoke the words directly toward the concrete floor, as if the weight of them coming out of her mouth were too heavy for her to hold up her head and face me. "What I do for sexual arousal and release is really unusual," she confessed. "To reach orgasm, I put on a diaper, then wet it or soil it."

I confess, she had me. I'd never heard of such a thing, although she went on to explain with a glimmer of hope in her eye that she'd discovered an online community of people who share the same fetish. Indeed, learning that you are not alone is often a healing discovery in and of itself.

I asked her how she felt about the situation and where she wanted to go with it from here. She paused, opened her mouth to speak, hesitated, and began trembling; then with tears cascading freely down her cheeks, she finally choked out the words: "How can I ever get married? What man is ever going to be okay with *this*?"

I asked Laura if she was willing to do some "soul work" with me to see if we couldn't figure out the origin of this behavior. As we began unpacking her history, I learned that Laura was the only child born to a single mom who had a major germ phobia. "I remember when I was about three years old, I fell off my tricycle and scraped my knee really badly. I went running into the house to find my mom, crying at the top of my lungs. I found her in the kitchen and held my arms out hoping to be picked up and comforted. But when my mom saw the blood gushing from my knee and all of the dirt smeared along my shin, she freaked out. She actually climbed up on the kitchen countertop just to get away from me."

"What happened after that, Laura? Who cleaned you up? Who comforted you?" Laura had no recollection. She only remembered that her mother was incapable of responding the way she needed her to. In fact, Laura had no memories of ever being held, cradled, or physically comforted by her mother. She did have memories, however, of lying in her crib for hours at a time, alone and helpless.

It didn't take a brain surgeon to make the connection. Obviously, the only warmth Laura experienced as a young child was when she wet or soiled her own diapers. To a baby who receives ample amounts of physical affection, the sensation of a dirty diaper can be rather disturbing. But to a baby who is never touched, the sensation of a wet or dirty diaper may be a welcome reprieve from the monotonous isolation he or she constantly feels. It's not difficult to imagine how this sensation would naturally evolve with a human being, translating into a sexual diaper fetish as an adult.

You might wonder, "What is a person to do with a situation like that? How does she heal?" Just as we learn new ways of behaving in life and relationships over time, I believe we can also learn new ways of responding to physical or sexual stimulus. Although many behavioral patterns are deeply ingrained, our brains are actually very pliable and open to receiving new information. I recommended that Laura find a support group of two or three other women with whom she could confide about her mother's lack of physical affection. She didn't necessarily have to reveal her diaper fetish if it was something that she felt uncomfortable sharing or if she feared making others feel uncomfortable. I challenged her to simply ask for what she needed most—physical touch. This could come in the form of frequent hugs, pats on the back, or the comforting caress of a pair of hands touching hers during times of prayer.

I would love to tell you that Laura completely overcame her fetish, got married to a wonderful man, had a houseful of kids, and lived happily ever after. I don't know that for sure. Once Laura graduated from the college where we met, we lost touch. While I would like to think that she benefited greatly from our conversations, I have since realized that *I* was the real beneficiary. This incredibly heavy secret that this precious young woman feared no one in the world could possibly understand, she entrusted to me. And I have carried it (and her) in my heart ever since.

Laura, if you are reading this, know that you are loved, and I think you are one of the bravest women I have ever met.

9

Putting Fantasy in Its Place

We have spent a great deal of time exposing the deeper meaning behind our sexual thoughts, particularly fantasies that are most confusing or dangerous. But before we wrap up our discussion completely, I would like to explore the deeper meaning behind our *healthy* sexual thoughts that lead to personal integrity and relational safety. Why? For the same reason that a bank teller is trained to recognize counterfeit bills not by examining counterfeits but by closely examining the *real* and the *genuine*.

We can think about fantasy as rehearsing for a play. Many of our fantasies are relatively unedited and can lead us into sexual compromise very quickly, especially given the vast number of sexually compromising situations we witness in the media. However, if we intentionally fantasize about how to nip an inappropriate entanglement in the bud and do the right thing early on, it will never blossom into a full-grown nightmare.

THE TEST OF MY TESTIMONY

I have been warned multiple times by multiple people: "Leading a ministry such as yours paints a big, red bull's-eye on your forehead!"

I have always known it to be true, yet I was still taken by surprise over the events that transpired on June 15, 2011. As it was all unfolding, I suspected that I would *need* to write about this eventually—both as therapy to process it for myself and, hopefully, as *preventive* therapy for my readers.

As I arrived at Dallas/Ft. Worth International Airport on June 14, I was informed that if I flew into Los Angeles, I might be stranded there for several days. A volcano in Chile had erupted, sending an ash cloud over New Zealand's airspace, which would prevent planes from heading in that direction any time soon. Due to speak in Christchurch, New Zealand, within seventy-two hours, I begged airport staff to let me on that plane in spite of the warnings. I knew my chances of getting to New Zealand would be much greater if I were already in LA than if I were still in Dallas.

When I arrived in LA, I learned that my New Zealand flight was canceled . . . indefinitely. Although "acts of God" usually mean that you are responsible for your own lodging, Qantas was kind enough to put all of us stranded travelers in a very nice Marriott hotel near LAX. I got settled into my room around 3:00 a.m., slept until 10:00 a.m., enjoyed a leisurely Starbucks breakfast, and then headed to the swimming pool for some exercise since I had almost twelve hours before the next possible flight left the United States. I felt as though I had been given a free twenty-four-hour California vacation, and I was soaking up every minute of it.

I was minding my own business in the shallow end of the pool when a handsome fortyish guy in jogging shorts, tank top, and iPod earbuds strolled by. He obviously had just completed a jog and was contemplating the hot tub. He asked how the water was, and I gave him the thumbs-up.

Casual conversation evolved so naturally I can't even remember what the first words spoken were. I eventually asked if he was also stuck in LA due to the ash cloud. Negative. He was a pilot on sabbatical until his next flight later that evening. He then asked why I was heading to New Zealand. I explained that I was an author doing a three-week speaking tour. Predictably, he asked, "What do you write and speak on?"

I gave my standard as-brief-as-possible answer so as not to bore him to death. "Healthy sexuality and spirituality."

Bored? Obviously not. Intrigued? Maybe. He replied, "So . . . if I read your book, I'll learn how to have better sex?"

Again, keeping it as brief as possible, I responded, "Well, if your wife reads my latest book, *The Sexually Confident Wife*, I guess she might learn a few things."

Sensing it was time to wrap up the conversation and move on, I wished him a good day and started swimming toward the opposite end of the enormous pool.

Mr. Pilot-Guy had been long forgotten in the 2.5 minutes it took me to reach the deep end. My mind was already in Christchurch, praying that the volcanic ash cloud would clear and that their recent earthquake aftershocks wouldn't prevent my plane from landing once I actually arrived.

Suddenly I hear a deep voice chuckle, "You're going to have to swim a lot faster than *that* to get any exercise!"

I look up to discover Mr. Pilot-Guy's toned and tanned frame casting a shadow over me in the California sunshine. He squats down, extends his arm for a formal handshake, and says, "I'm Kyle [not his real name, of course], and I was thinking it would be great to have lunch with you. You seem like a really interesting person, and I'd love to get to know you. So . . . what do you think?"

I can't recall ever being at a loss for words in my entire life, but color me speechless in that moment. "Well . . . uh . . . I . . . uh . . . I don't know if I'd really have time."

He interrupted my stammering to rescue us both from the awkwardness. "Look, I have to eat anyway, and I'd love to eat *with you*. I'll be in the hotel lobby at 12:30. If you're there, great. I think we'd have a really good time together. If you're not there, well, I understand."

My crushing reply? "Uh, okay."

And then I swam away in the other direction with a million thoughts ricocheting through my brain. Well, maybe just seven thoughts. Seven thoughts that I'd like to share with you as to why I had no desire to turn this common fantasy into what I knew would become a painful reality. (After all, what woman *hasn't* fantasized about being found attractive and desirable company to a handsome stranger in an exotic location with nothing but time on her hands and no one present to hold her accountable?)

1. I have other things I'm more passionate about.

As much as I'd love to tell you that my first mental response to Kyle's lunch invitation was totally God-centered and super-spiritual, I confess that it was not. My very *first* thought? Honestly? (Promise not to laugh or think less of me!) My knee-jerk reaction was, "I just got in this pool! And if I had to choose between a leisurely lunch with an overly attentive, handsome pilot or continue swimming for ninety more minutes in the California sunshine, I'll keep swimming, thank you very much."

You may not love swimming like I do, but my point is that when you fill your life *full* of things that you absolutely *love* doing, it's much easier to stay on the right track when temptation comes knocking.

Think about it. One of the main reasons men and women get so sidetracked by inappropriate emotional entanglements is that their lives are way out of balance. On one extreme, we can fill our days with all kinds of stresses and pressures, but that kind of pressure-cooker environment makes human beings very susceptible to releasing those pressures in some pretty inappropriate ways. On the opposite extreme, we can also let our days become so boring and mundane that we are tempted to spice things up with something way out of the ordinary, such as an extramarital fling.

But what if we created a life that positively fueled us—emotionally, mentally, spiritually, physically, sexually? Would we feel the need for that affair when the opportunity comes knocking? I didn't. I didn't feel the need at all. Thank You, God, that I didn't feel *any* need for anything more than what I had already been given in that moment!

God has given me such a feeling of purpose and meaning—in my ministry, in marriage, in motherhood, in special me-time moments, such as swimming, sipping Chai tea, nibbling dark chocolate, or lighting a candle and staring at the flame, as I count my blessings—that an afternoon lunch affair couldn't possibly pull me away from my true passions. Is your life filled with so many healthy passions that you don't have the time, energy, or inclination for any unhealthy passions to develop?

2. I refuse to trust people more than I trust my God-given instinct.

Okay, so my next thought after *Gee, I'd really rather keep swimming!* was, *What's this guy's real motive here?* I mean, sure, Kyle could have had the purest of motives—absolutely nothing on his mind but an innocent conversation over a leisurely lunch. And Elvis may actually be resurrected from the dead and hiding out in various Dunkin' Donuts shops around the country . . . and my Maltese puppy may give birth to a litter of humpback whales while I'm in New Zealand—humpback whales that are able to swallow the Pacific Ocean in one gulp.

Seriously, I guess there is a slight chance that "just lunch" was all he had in mind. But why take that risk? He could also have had a lot of *other* things on his mind, things like getting a big fat ego stroke, a feather in his cap, a notch in his belt, and so on. In the words of my friend Terrica, "Oh, he totally was hitting on you! Pilots are famous for their traveling trysts! I know one and he's always talking about how pilots get so much a-a-a-a-ction!" I also realized that the situation could be far more dangerous and have a lot more at stake than just falling into a hotel room romance (as if that isn't bad enough). I'm no dummy. I realized that Kyle may have been a clean-cut, handsome guy with personality plus, but so was Ted Bundy—you know, lawyer by day, serial killer by night. And for all I knew, Kyle was only *posing* as a pilot. He was wearing jogging shorts, not a uniform. I didn't ask to see his badge or ID, not that he couldn't have crafted those things himself. While he may have the personality of Ryan Seacrest, he could also have the mentality of Jack the Ripper. Glad I didn't hang around to find out.

So before you decide to let some sweet-talking eye candy lure you into some sort of compromising situation, think of someone like Natalee Holloway. I am sure at some point she certainly wished she had never left that Aruban nightclub with those three men. And so do her grieving parents. And so do we. What happens to women at the hands of sick and twisted men is more than a crime. It is absolutely heinous.

And the only way to try and prevent something similar from happening to *us* is to trust our God-given instincts.

3. I realize when I'm trying to rationalize stupidity.

It wouldn't have taken much justification to press through the warning flags and "just do lunch" with Kyle. I could have easily entertained thoughts such as:

- *As long as we stay in a public place, it'll be okay. There's no real danger in meeting him in the lobby restaurant.*
- *It will be one hour, two at most. That's not enough time to be unfaithful to my husband.*
- *No one at this hotel knows who I am, so it's not like I'm going to get caught.*
- *This may be God opening a door for me to talk to Kyle about Jesus! (Yes, we Christians often use evangelism as an excuse to follow our flesh.)*

Fortunately this was *not* my thought pattern this time, although fifteen to twenty years ago, I'm pretty sure it would have been. Praise God for transformation!

The thoughts that were rolling through my head regarding the logic of such a lunch date were more like:

- *Okay, let's say I agree to one lunch. What then? A yearning for another lunch in another city someday! And another! And then lunch won't be enough!*
- *Why stir up insatiable yearnings that ultimately lead to Heartbreak Hotel when I can just mind my own business here at the Marriott and keep my heart intact?*
- *You know one hour of conversation will not scratch his itch (or yours if you start this thing). It will be like scratching poison ivy, making it itch even more, causing it to spread and do even more damage!*
- *If you give him an inch, he's going to want a mile. If you give him the*

impression that you're friends now, he's going to start contacting you whenever he wants an ego stroke.

- *Do you really want to be some pilot's little plaything?*
- *There may be no getting rid of him afterward. He'll want to exchange cell phone numbers or start e-mailing you.*
- *He could easily become a leech, sucking more and more life out of you with each contact.*

You get the idea. Sometimes women can easily romanticize the notion of such an innocent-yet-intimate rendezvous with a handsome stranger in an exotic location, but, sweet pea, this ain't Hollywood, nor is it a Harlequin romance novel.

This is real life, where people get hurt, hearts get ripped out and stomped on, marriages get damaged (sometimes beyond repair), and children get caught in the crossfire and wonder, *What in the world happened to our family?* Not going there. I'm just not going there. I hope you won't go there, either.

One of my favorite sayings has become, "Don't stick your head into the lion's mouth before praying 'Lord, save me from the lion!'" A much better strategy is not to go into the lion's den at all. Then you don't have to worry about getting devoured. "Be alert and of sober mind. Your enemy the devil prowls around like a roaring lion looking for someone to devour" (1 Peter 5:8 NIV).

4. God's grace *is* sufficient!

In those split seconds of swimming away from Kyle, I sensed I was not alone, and I'm not just referring to the outgoing, handsome pilot standing there. I could feel the Holy Spirit deep in the fibers of my being, washing me with wisdom as I freestyled my way back toward the shallow end.

I was quickly reminded of where I came from many years ago (a deep pit of desperation and compromise as a love- and sex-addicted teenager), where I was now (walking in victory and helping thousands of others do the same), and where I was heading (toward even greater levels of spiritual intimacy with my heavenly Bridegroom, both in this life and in the next).

Of course, Satan was also trying to get a few words in edgewise. *Why not just go for it?! Sample a little forbidden fruit. It's been a long time, and who knows if you'll ever have this kind of opportunity again? No one is going to know. Come on; live a little! After all, God is not going to love you any less. Remember? His mercies are new every morning!* (Yes, Satan knows Scripture and will use it as a weapon against us if we're not careful!)

Whether God would love me or not if I took such a big step backward has never been a concern for me. He loved me in the midst of my deepest, darkest, most secretive moments. Is there any depth, any level of darkness, any secret that would cause Him to love me less? Not a chance. "*Nothing* . . . will ever be able to separate us from the love of God" (Rom. 8:38–39 NCV, emphasis mine). That passage means exactly what it says—*nothing* could change God's love for us. *Absolutely nothing!* Zip! Zilch! Nada! Not one thing. Not even one million things!

Sure. God would *not* love me any less. And His mercies *are* new every morning. But why would I want to go around this same stupid mountain again when I was already living in the promised land? Why put shackles back around my soul when I'd already been set free? It just didn't make sense to me, and I'm thankful for that knowledge. It wasn't always there.

Even the best of Christians stumble into sin on occasion, but sincere followers of Christ don't use God's mercy as a license to do stupid things or live dangerously. Sin *is* easily forgiven, but the price that Christ paid for my sin was far too high for me to just sin without second thought.

Yes, God would indeed forgive me. But as freely as God gives us mercy in our time of need, He also gives us grace in our time of need.

What's the difference? Mercy is God's ability to forgive our sins *after* we have committed them. Grace is God's power to avoid that sin in the first place. I couldn't ignore the grace that I felt flowing directly out of my intimate relationship with Jesus in those speechless moments of shock and surprise. Yes, mercy would be there if I needed it, but grace was there first. *Grace was there first.* And I welcomed her with open arms.

Jesus may as well have been wading in the shallow end, eavesdropping on the conversation, watching anxiously to see if I'd be slipping out of the pool and into the shower to get ready for my rendezvous with Kyle, or if I'd continue enjoying this special little preconference retreat time He'd carved out for me.

He knew what I'd choose. He has taught me well. Basking in His lavish love is *so* much more intoxicating than the attentions of any other man.

Are you so completely satisfied through your intimate relationship with Jesus that humans pale in comparison?

5. Reality is better than fantasy.

In addition to realizing what amazingly unconditional love God has for me even if I were to choose lunch with Kyle over swimming with Jesus, I also thought of my husband at home. And although I preach endlessly against making comparisons, I did go there. Only because I knew that Greg would come out smelling like a freshly plucked rose.

Kyle struck up a simple conversation. Greg struck me more than twenty years ago as a man I simply couldn't live without.

Kyle had extended his hand with interest. Greg had asked for my hand in marriage.

Kyle was offering a single lunch. Greg has offered me his entire life.

Kyle was willing to give me the time of day. Greg is willing to give me all the days he has remaining.

Kyle may have wanted a little afternoon delight, no strings attached. Greg wants to delight me every afternoon he can, and he doesn't mind the strings at all.

Kyle wanted to lead me down a dangerous detour. Greg wants to lead me down life's path with honor, dignity, and integrity.

Kyle was in search of stirring up some relational intensity. Greg is in search of stirring up genuine intimacy.

Sure, Greg has his flaws. His introverted nature can drive this social butterfly a little stir-crazy at times. He leaves whisker shavings on the bathroom counter and dirty dishes in the kitchen sink on occasion. He snores. He forgets. He doesn't read my mind and doesn't do things the same way I would. But he's there. He's there every day, longing for my love; he's there every night, happy to do nothing more than sleep in bed next to me if sleeping is all I have energy to do.

He loves me. This flawed man daily chooses to love this flawed woman. And I feel like the luckiest girl on the planet.

Conclusion: Why would I jeopardize the startling beauty of the life we have built together? Why would I want a hamburger when I have prime rib at home? It just wouldn't make sense. In fact, it would be sheer stupidity.

Even if you don't think your marriage is anything to shout about today, it certainly has that potential *tomorrow*. There is always hope for a marriage miracle, and God is an expert in that very business. So, ladies, before you let some sweet-talking stranger or any other person woo you into stroking his ego (or any other body part), remember the weeks and months your husband pursued you with honest intentions; the years he has worked hard to provide a good life for his family; the overwhelming (sometimes paralyzing) desire he carries in his heart to prove himself worthy of your love; the multiple ways he teaches your children what it means to be loved by a father, by *the* Father; and how desperately the little boy trapped inside that grown man's body longs to be affirmed and respected by the special woman that he has dreamed of, longed for, prayed over, and pledged his entire life.

Gentlemen, remember how your wife has given up all other romantic possibilities to love and serve *you*; the years she has taken such pride in caring for you, your children, and the home you share together; and how desperately the little girl trapped inside that grown woman's body longs to be cherished and celebrated by the special man that she has dreamed of, longed for, prayed over, and pledged her entire life.

By either putting fantasies in their place or indulging carelessly in them, *you* hold the power to make or break your marriage and family.

I hope you'll choose to make it.

6. An affair isn't what I really want.

I have been reading a book called *The Broken Image*, by Leanne Payne,[1] and she uses two words together that have jolted me awake with their truer combined meaning.

First word: *genital*

Second word: *intimacy*

Genital intimacy. Obviously it means the physical touching of an area of the human body that is intended to be pleasured by (and provide pleasure to) another human being. *One* human being. Not your boyfriend or girlfriend, your lover, or even your fiancé, but your one lawfully wedded spouse.

I envision a movie theater ticket stub that boldly states "ADMIT ONE."

That is what God intended. Not one-until-you're-tired-of-him or one-after-another but simply one. How I wish I had understood that thirty years ago before many premarital regrets were conceived.

Why would God design our minds, hearts, and bodies in such a way that we thrive in relationship with one but can utterly destroy ourselves in relationship with multiples of one? Could it be that God, when He designed human beings in His image, created us to be "jealous" (wanting someone all to ourselves rather than sharing) because He is a jealous God? (See Exod. 34:14; Deut. 4:24.)

Ironically, on the day I first began journaling about this California Dreaming experience, I completed the reading of the book *One Thousand Gifts* by my dear friend Ann Voskamp, which is about how she learned to count her blessings and lavishly give thanks to the Giver of all gifts. I am startled, yet stirred, by the passion in her pen as she writes:

> God—He has blessed—caressed.
>
> *I could bless God*—caress with thanks.
>
> It's our making love.
>
> God makes love with grace upon grace, every moment a making of His love for us. And He invites the turning over of the hand, the opening and saying the Yes with thanks. Then God lays down all of His fullness into all the emptiness. I am in Him. He is in me. I embrace God in the moment, I give Him thanks and *I bless God* and we meet and couldn't I make love to God, making every moment love for Him? To know Him the way Adam knew Eve. Spirit skin to spirit skin.
>
> This is what His love means. I want it: *union*.[2]

Wow. Almost makes you blush with anticipation, doesn't it? The very thought that we are designed by God as the *fulfillment* of

His deepest longings—to be in relationship with, in communication with, in communion with, in love with Him. He in love with us, and we in love with Him.

And if we are created in His very image, this explains why we feel so compelled to fully experience loving, intimate relationships. We crave them in the fibers of our being, like we crave air and water.

Only we sometimes get it wrong. So very wrong.

Rather than look for love in relationship with the God who created us and the spouses He blesses us with, we assume that's simply not enough. Like Adam and Eve, we want more, failing to realize that more—something other than what we've been lovingly allotted—*isn't* better. In fact, it's *bad* for us.

But the problem isn't in the wanting. Even God wants intimacy. The problem is where we look for it, what we settle for.

We have misguided passions and misguided gratitude. For example, would it make sense for us to be filled with a heart full of gratitude for a gift that God has given and then turn and offer thanks to another god completely? Of course not. But how many men and women are stirred by God to be sexually intimate with the one God has given yet turn and share that passion with another "one" entirely? Rather than channel those sexual and emotional yearnings in the ordained direction we have been given (called marriage), some open themselves to another.

And most usually grow to regret it within a very short time. One man I know thought the grass was greener and the sky bluer on the other side of his marriage fence. So he divorced and married the woman who wooed him over to her side of that fence. And then he discovered that she had given him much more than he had bargained for, including herpes and thousands of dollars' worth of debt he wasn't aware of when he made his decisions in the heat of all those moments together.

Or a young woman who mistakenly assumed that she wanted sex (genital intimacy) with an old high-school flame, when all she really wanted was a listening ear and some encouragement to work through the abundance of emotional baggage she had dragged into her marriage. Turns out, the "other one" wasn't interested in her baggage, only her body.

But regardless of how many times we've gotten it wrong in the past, we can allow our sexuality to be fully sanctified by our spirituality. We can develop such an overwhelming appetite for healthy fruit that forbidden fruit loses its appeal altogether.

7. *One* is all I need.

All of this contemplation about the connection between spirituality and sexuality has led me to this ultimate conclusion about why I didn't go there with that pilot who invited me to have lunch: *Why would I want to share myself with another "one" when I've already been given "the One" by God?*

To climb down off the high spiritual plane and put it into practical, earthly terms, Greg knows me. Knows every stretch mark, every dimple. Knows what turns me on, what turns me off, what I fantasize about, and where I draw the line. He pushes my buttons, not my envelope. My "one" knows me sexually, satisfies me sexually, and celebrates me sexually. I don't need to be known in such a way by another.

One is all I need, all I desire. And my one shares my last name, my address, my children, my bank accounts, my bed, my dreams, my goals for our future together. My one shares my passions, especially my passion for the God who longs for us to be one with Him.

Perhaps you don't feel nearly as strong a sexual or spiritual connection with your spouse today. There have been many days over the past twenty-three years that I didn't either or that Greg didn't. Regardless of where your marriage is today, know that there is always hope for your future—as long as you are looking to God to guide you on your path toward deeper levels of sexual and spiritual connection.

BEHIND THE CURTAIN: FREE AT LAST!

Lilly had struggled for years with inappropriate fantasies and dreams about being in prison and subjected to sexual seduction and rape at the hands of the other prisoners, both male and female. These images had brought great confusion, guilt, and shame since her teenage years—that is, until she asked God to either take away this fantasy completely or give her deeper wisdom and insight about what it actually means in her own mind.

"God, what is my brain trying to heal itself *from* with this distorted recurring dream?" Lilly prayed.

As the only child of a single mother, Lilly had never been sexually abused. She wasn't exposed to pornography until early adulthood, and she felt no draw to continue in that direction once she became aware of it. In her early thirties, Lilly wasn't married and had never had sex. So I could see why this dream was so bewildering to her.

We began paying closer attention to the details of the dream. I asked her to describe the prison cell, what the inmates were like who pursued her sexually, how she felt about the experience, and so on. Interestingly, once she gave careful consideration to such details, certain things stood out to her. Her prison cell wasn't just a single bunk with a concrete floor and gray walls. It had carpet on the floor and curtains on the windows and a frilly bedspread on the double bed, yet there were still iron bars separating her from the rest of the prison.

"Describe to me how you felt growing up, Lilly. What was the emotion that surfaced most often in your day-to-day existence?" I asked.

Lilly responded, "I remember wishing like crazy that my mother would get married and have more children because I desperately wanted brothers and sisters. But that never happened."

"And do you remember what emotion being an only child elicited in you? Were you lonely? Bored? Depressed?" I inquired.

"I was definitely all those things, but more than anything I think I felt *responsible* for my mother's emotional health. Since she was without a husband or other children, I grew up knowing that *I* was her only source of real connection with another human being, and the weight of that responsibility felt suffocating at times. I didn't go out with my friends many evenings or weekends simply because I thought it would be cruel to leave my mother at home alone," she recalled.

"Did your mother communicate to you, either overtly or covertly, that she had this expectation of you? Or did *you* put this expectation on *yourself?*" I challenged. (I felt it incredibly important to clarify whether this was a decision made by choice or by emotional manipulation.)

Pondering the question for a few moments, she replied, "I can't think of a single way that my mom would have given me that impression. It's just always been an assumption that I made, I guess . . . or perhaps it was really an excuse, with my introverted personality, not to have to venture out and be social."

"What would 'venturing out and being social' mean to you, Lilly? What would that have required of you?"

"That I get over my fear of people and my fear of being around them. I guess I masked that fear behind being a social martyr for the sake of my mother's well-being."

"Why was being around other people such a scary proposition for you?"

"I just wasn't very socially skilled. I felt awkward around people; I *still* do! I've always felt stupid when I can't think of anything to say in conversation. That's probably why my mother forced me to go to public school, so I could maybe conquer my shyness," she considered. "But I don't know how much good it did. I'm still pretty shy."

"So in light of how you felt as a child and how this feeling persists in adulthood, is it possible that your dream is merely a symbol of the 'mental prison' you've lived in your whole life?" I asked.

She didn't toy with the idea for long before nodding in agreement that this was a very distinct possibility. "And could this mental picture also be a representation of how you've often chosen not to get out of the house and experience other people, so you've unconsciously longed for them to come to you?"

Again, more positive nodding. "For people to pursue me is always my preference because I don't have the courage to pursue them. But I don't want them to try to have sex with me! That's just crazy!" she exclaimed.

Lilly was getting the idea. *Sex with prison inmates* was *not* what she wanted for her future. But she couldn't ignore how the recurring manifestation of this fantasy in her dreams must surely symbolize something much deeper. It symbolized her loneliness, her desperation for human connection, her paralyzing fear over the possibility of having to pursue friendships, her concern that anyone on the planet would ever find her and want to usher her out of the mental prison of being her mother's only playmate. She feared *becoming* her mother, only without her own child to connect with.

Once these fears were acknowledged, we began strategizing how Lilly could find friends and create deeper relationships than what her job as a bank teller allowed. She became active in a local church with a large adult singles group, and she also began volunteering with Habitat for Humanity. "Making friends is a lot easier when there's a common goal you can focus on. Swapping life stories with people while swinging hammers and painting walls together isn't nearly as difficult as sitting in Starbucks over coffee thinking, *What am I going to say next?*"

The prison fantasy invaded her dreams far less often, which was a huge relief to Lilly. But believe it or not, one night she had a similar dream, only the details were much different:

> I was lying on my bed in the prison cell, but this time the other male and female inmates weren't being allowed in my room to have sex with me. Instead, they were being kept out by a particular prison guard who looked at me through the bars with such compassion. But after seeing how lonely I'd become in my prison cell all by myself, he began letting himself in and crawling into my bed with me. He didn't try to seduce me or be inappropriate at all. He just held me tightly, comforting me with his strong protection.
>
> This continued night after night. In fact, he began working the day shift, and instead of going home after clocking out, he'd come to my cell and spend every night with me. So he was watching out for me both night and day. I felt like I had my own personal bodyguard.
>
> Then came the day that I learned I was being let out of prison on parole. I was filled with such mixed emotions. On the one hand, I wanted out of that cell like crazy! I wanted to experience the world I'd been locked away from for so long! But the thought of not having this prison guard in my world twenty-four/seven shook me to the core. I simply didn't want to leave him.

On the day of my release, I was escorted to an awaiting taxicab by two guards—one was the man who'd kept me company all this time, and the other was someone I didn't recognize. The back door was opened for me, and I climbed in without a glance because I couldn't bear to let the guards see me crying over the thought of having to leave—not the *place,* but the *person* I'd fallen in love with.

Then I saw this man remove his badge and unfasten his key ring. Handing them to his partner, he walked around to the other side of the cab and climbed in! He was leaving the prison to continue being my personal bodyguard, my constant companion!

And that is when I finally recognized this man.

Jesus. He'd held me in my captivity, and now He would walk with me in my freedom.

Jesus is *always* near. Regardless of what kind of mental prison you have been in, regardless of the fantasies or dreams that invade your mind, regardless of the sexual thoughts you (or those you love) have been enslaved by, know that our sovereign Lord is always there to help you understand them, to protect you from them, and to comfort you through them.

Conclusion

The Rest of the Story

I opened this book with a vivid dream I experienced toward the beginning of the writing process, but I intentionally stopped midstream. In Paul Harvey fashion, now I'll share the "rest of the story."

Just when I thought I'd pretty much solved the mystery about the meaning of the two lions—that surely the message of the dream was not to be too legalistic or too liberal about our sexual thoughts—I realized there were other clues in the dream that had yet to be recognized or woven in. I remembered that, in the dream, I was standing by myself in a ripened wheat field. But why a wheat field? Why not a rose garden? Or a stretch of beach? Or a mountaintop or under a shade tree?

Because the wheat field had significance. In John 4:35 we see Jesus teaching His disciples: "You have a saying, 'Four more months till harvest.' But I tell you, open your eyes and look at the fields ready for harvest now" (NCV).

Jesus is using the harvest field as a word picture to illustrate how there are lost souls ready to be saved, and He's commissioning *us* to gather them in and lead them into His eternal kingdom! In fact, He challenges His disciples that they need to pray for even more workers to bring in the harvest:

> When he saw the crowds, he felt sorry for them because they were hurting and helpless, like sheep without a shepherd. Jesus said to his followers, "There are many people to harvest but only a few workers to help harvest them. Pray to the Lord, who owns the harvest, that he will send more workers to gather his harvest." (Matt. 9:36–38 NCV)

Notice the reason Matthew tells us that Jesus longed to bring the harvest in (or draw the people closer to Himself): because they were *hurting* and *helpless*. That describes a lot of us, both inside and outside the church, doesn't it?

But of course, wheat is also used in a different (less desirable) context in the Bible. In Luke 22:31–32 Jesus warns Simon Peter: "Satan has asked to test all of you as a farmer sifts his wheat. I have prayed that you will not lose your faith! Help your brothers be stronger when you come back to me" (NCV).

To be sifted like wheat would mean that before Peter and the disciples could become even more effective for God, they had to face further challenges. New level, new devil. Satan wanted to test them for the sole purpose of weeding them out and rendering them useless.

So there again, my dream had a dual meaning. I could break away from both extremes of legalism and liberalism and actually be free to do what I was there to do—harvest the wheat field (by writing books because that is how God has gifted me to "harvest" or pursue people for His sake). Or I could allow both extremes of legalism and liberalism to keep my hands occupied, too distracted to focus on the established work. As a result I would be allowing Satan to "sift me like wheat," rendering me useless to the expansion of God's kingdom.

Finally, I remembered that in the dream I was wearing a white dress, which is so unlike me. I am more of a "blue jeans, T-shirt, and ball cap" kind of girl, so I knew there had to be some significance to the white flowing dress. Then it hit me. When do you see a woman wearing a white flowing dress? On her wedding day, of course. The girl in the dream wasn't just *me*. She was a bride. But not just any bride. She was the bride of Christ, which is symbolic language for saying "all of us believers in Jesus."

In Revelation 19:6–9 we read what's in store for all of us who've chosen to put our faith in Jesus Christ as Lord and Savior:

> Then I heard what sounded like a great multitude, like the roar of rushing waters and like loud peals of thunder, shouting:
>
> *"Hallelujah!*
> *For our Lord God Almighty reigns.*
> *Let us rejoice and be glad*
> *and give him glory!*
> *For the wedding of the Lamb has come,*
> *and his bride has made herself ready.*
> *Fine linen, bright and clean,*
> *was given her to wear."*
>
> (Fine linen stands for the righteous acts of God's holy people.)
>
> Then the angel said to me, "Write this: Blessed are those who are invited to the wedding supper of the Lamb!" And he added, "These are the true words of God." (NIV)

Did you catch that? When Jesus returns for us, just as He promised He would, He's returning not as merely a Master to

His slaves, a Savior to the lost, a Friend to the lonely, or a Father to His children. He's returning as a heavenly Bridegroom for His beloved bride! There's going to be a grand and glorious wedding, and you and I are invited—not just as a guest, but as the bride! *We are collectively the bride of Christ!*[1]

This dream wasn't just about *me*, but about all believers. We need to take our roles seriously—as the "bride of Christ," as the "gatherers of the harvest," as the voices of reason in a sexually unreasonable world—to help bind up the brokenhearted and help them look for love, not in all the *wrong* places, but in the *right* place, through a more intimate relationship with our Creator God, and through healthier relationships with themselves and others.

But the most serious role we have in life is to represent God well, both as spiritual beings and as sexual beings. We need to remember that our sexuality is a beautiful gift from God and is as unique as our own fingerprints, that sexual confusion comes part and parcel with being human, that sexual fantasies are perfectly normal, but *we can* control them rather than let them control us.

And we need to remember that God doesn't just speak to us through sermons or scriptures. Just as He did in biblical times, He often speaks to us through dreams while we are asleep or through our thoughts and fantasies while we are wide awake.

The main question is, are we listening?

Appendix 1

Ten Excuses that Turn Fantasies into Painful Realities

As a life/relationship coach I've had the privilege of working with some of the most respectable people you'd ever want to meet. These are not rapists on skid row or crack-peddling prostitutes. They are accomplished doctors, ministers, missionaries, businessmen and businesswomen, home-room mothers, chancel choir directors, and so on.

But regardless of how upstanding we can appear in our public roles, we're never exempt from downward-spiraling behaviors. Part of my coaching with individuals and couples is to help them recognize specific thought patterns that opened the door for their once-fanciful dream to morph into their most recent nightmare.

Fantasies don't become realities without a little premeditation and selfish action on our part, so let's look at ten excuses that can lead us toward a moment of pleasure but a lifetime of pain.

1. I deserve time off for good behavior.

Time off for good behavior is for prisoners on parole. Marriage isn't a prison but a privilege. I doubt that time off for good behavior was part of the vows you took or the marriage contract you signed, so don't use this lame excuse to justify behavior that will ultimately bring great shame and humiliation to you, your spouse, and your family for generations to come.

2. **It's now or never . . .**

   My daddy always told me that if someone is looking to strike a business deal with you, and it's a "now or never" option, *always* choose never. It's not just a good policy in business deals, but also in avoiding relational monkey business.

3. **As long as we're here . . .**

   As long as we're at home in our normal surroundings, going about our normal routine doesn't seem like such a challenge. But when we take a little trip and step into a new place, out of eyesight or earshot of friends and family, we can quickly lose our relational bearings. That's why business travelers have a particularly challenging lifestyle, and also why vacationing alone or without a spouse can open the door to compromise quickly. Make sure to keep your guard *way* up whenever you're away from home.

4. **Acting out this fantasy will make me feel more desirable.**

   For a moment, perhaps. Although, chances are the fantasy will turn out much better than the reality. But even if it does float your boat big time, then what? You might come home feeling a little sexier for the few hours/days that your head remains in the clouds, but reality sets in like a bullet through the brain. If you want to avoid that kind of trauma, avoid the tryst.

5. No one has to know.

You're right. No one *has* to know; however, spouses (and even kids) have an uncanny knack for figuring these things out. But even if you manage to pull the wool over other people's eyes, *you'll* know. And your ruminating over it (positively or negatively) can constantly draw your attention away from where it needs to be—on your spouse, children, house, job, church, and so on. Allowing a fantasy to become a reality is like renting out your brain to the person involved. And like renters from hell, sometimes they refuse to leave when you're ready to have your brain back.

6. He or she is not my cup of tea anyway.

When my coaching clients describe a person as "no one they'd ever be attracted to," I can see the end of the story coming a mile away. They are suddenly bewildered to find that they were *wrong*. By letting their guard down around this not-so-desirable person, they have come to desire that individual intensely. Just because you don't feel an attraction to someone immediately doesn't mean that an attraction couldn't develop over time and a few cups of coffee, so be wise and steer as clear as necessary to keep even future temptation at bay.

7. If loving you is wrong, I don't wanna be right!

Love is not only blind but also deaf and dumb. Or, more accurately, feeling like you might be "in love" causes you to see only what you want to see. Hear only what you want to hear. Say only what you want to say. Even though you know in your head that this relationship is so wrong, your heart convinces you, "Oh, but it feels so right!" Wake up. Love is not a feeling. It is a commitment to truth (1 Cor. 13:6) and to your spouse's highest good (Eph. 5). So if this "fantasy relationship" isn't good for your spouse, it's especially not good for you.

8. What's good for the goose is good for the gander.

Some try to turn a fantasy into a reality in order to even the score. No doubt that the sting of a spouse's betrayal is sharp, but two wrongs do not make a right. Remember that hurting people hurt people. Focus on helping your spouse recognize the hurts that led him or her to be unfaithful in the first place, rather than grabbing a free pass and diving into the deep waters of dysfunction along with your spouse.

9. Do that to me one more time!

What's one more? That's how dieters fall off the weight-loss bandwagon, how smokers stay hooked on cigarettes, and how alcoholics remain enslaved to a shot glass. It is also how sex, love, and relationship addicts remain entrenched in emotional entanglements. If this describes you, adopt a new motto: The *last time* was the *last time*!

10. I can always repent later.

Let's face it. Love is a many splendored thing but can also be a very splintered thing, especially outside the boundaries of a marriage relationship. It gets under the surface of our skin, wreaks all kinds of havoc, and is incredibly hard to eradicate. Repenting of an inappropriate relationship sooner rather than later minimizes your chances of infection, so don't put off until tomorrow what you should have done yesterday.

Appendix 2

Curing the Sexual Abuse Epidemic

Now that you understand a great deal more about the origins of sexual fantasies, it is probably no surprise to you that those who fantasize about sexually abusing someone most likely have been sexually abused themselves. That is why I would like to call your attention to a few facts about this destructive epidemic.

1 in 4 girls and 1 in 6 boys will be sexually abused before their eighteenth birthday.[1]

That's 20 percent of our population. Although it's more comfortable to think of child sexual abuse in terms of "stranger danger," it's a fallacy that child molesters are strangers to our children. In fact, child molesters appear most often in our inner circles.

30 to 40 percent of the time children are abused by a family member.[2] **Another 50 percent are abused by someone the child knows and trusts.**[3]

Even if we can accept that abusers are people we know, we tend to hold onto the image of a middle-aged man as the typical child molester. While men make up the largest portion of the population of child molesters, we won't be in a position to truly protect children or effectively support survivors in our lives until we realize that child molesters can also be women and other children.

8 percent of abuse happens at the hands of the child's biological mother.[4] 40 percent of the time the abuser is an older or larger child.[5]

There are more than 39 million survivors of child sexual abuse in America,[6] and from them experts have documented the signs that appear in children after abuse, as well as behavioral patterns that appear *before* abuse occurs. So with the right training we can recognize when children are in danger and how to put boundaries in place to directly reduce the risk of abuse in our homes, neighborhoods, and youth-serving organizations.

Child sexual abuse is predictable and preventable, and we *all* play a part in the solution.

Keeping the secret and living a lie isolate survivors and perpetuate self-sabotaging behaviors, including trust and intimacy issues, bad boundaries, excessive drug and alcohol use, eating disorders, sexual promiscuity, and even crime. If you are a survivor, you understand the impact sexual abuse can have on your life—emotionally, physically, and spiritually. Know that you are not alone, it was not your fault, and you have the power to shift the blame back to where it belongs—on your abuser.

To Report Child Abuse

Call 911 or your local Child Protection Services agency or call 1-800-4-A-CHILD if you suspect abuse and need to talk it through.

To Learn What You Can Do to Prevent Abuse or Find Resources for Healing

Visit www.taalk.org or call 1-888-808-6558.

If You or Someone You Know Struggles with Inappropriate Feelings Toward Children

Visit www.stopitnow.org or call 1-888-PREVENT.

Appendix 3

Providing a Spiritual and Sexual Safe Haven

Are you a church leader looking for practical ways to demonstrate that you are a safe place for sexually broken people to seek guidance, encouragement, and support?

- Carefully consider those whom God has led to be a part of your congregation. Are there folks who have overcome sexual challenges, addictions, extramarital affairs, and so forth? Would they be willing to share a personal testimony about what God has done in their lives, marriages, or families? If so, give them an opportunity to let their light shine! It will be a great ray of hope to guide others! (If you are worried about the content of such a testimony, consider videotaping a two-way conversation between you and that person or couple, interview-style, which will allow for careful editing.)
- Ask a licensed professional counselor to speak in youth, college, and adult Sunday school classes about the unique sexual challenges we all face at various stages of life,

demonstrating approachability and a willingness to discuss such sensitive topics. Perhaps the speaker can also provide a list of local counseling resources for further exploration by those who feel the need to connect with someone outside the church altogether.

- Sex and Love Addicts Anonymous (www.slaafws.org) and Celebrate Recovery (www.celebraterecovery.com) support groups are ministries so worthy of extending to the community. Granted, many in your congregation would prefer to be a part of the sexual support group across town for anonymity's sake, but that's okay. Those from the other side of town can find anonymity and comfort in your congregation.
- Consider hosting a PureHOPE seminar or conference for your local community. PureHOPE is a ministry dedicated to providing Christian solutions in a sexualized culture, working collaboratively with churches and Christian schools to equip believers to Pray, Understand, Resolve, and Engage with culture to encourage a PURE lifestyle. Visit www.purehope.net for more information.
- Consider partnering with XXXchurch.com to host a "Porn Sunday" Event. The focus of the weekend service is to get churches talking about the "elephant in the pew" and get help for people who are struggling with porn and sex addiction. More than six hundred churches from all over the world have participated in this event throughout the years, and the resources and video from the 2011 event are available to your church to be used any time you want, for free. Go to www.XXXchurch.com to learn more.
- Offer an entire weekend conference focusing on healthy sexuality, including keynote speakers and workshops on a wide variety of topics that will minister to teens, college

students, single adults, married couples, and parents. (For more information on having Shannon speak at your youth, women's, or marriage conference, go to www.ShannonEthridge.com/speaking.)

Appendix 4

Twelve Steps to Recovery[1]

1. We admitted we were powerless over our addictions and compulsive behaviors, that our lives had become unmanageable.
I know that nothing good lives in me, that is, in my sinful nature. For I have the desire to do what is good, but I cannot carry it out. (Rom. 7:18)

2. We came to believe that a power greater than ourselves could restore us to sanity.
For it is God who works in you to will and to act according to his good purpose. (Phil. 2:13)

3. We made a decision to turn our lives and our wills over to the care of God.
Therefore, I urge you, brothers, in view of God's mercy, to offer your bodies as living sacrifices, holy and pleasing to God—this is your spiritual act of worship. (Rom. 12:1)

4. We made a searching and fearless moral inventory of ourselves.
Let us examine our ways and test them, and let us return to the LORD. *(Lam. 3:40)*

5. We admitted to God, to ourselves, and to another human being the exact nature of our wrongs.
Therefore confess your sins to each other and pray for each other so that you may be healed. (James 5:16)

6. We were entirely ready to have God remove all these defects of character.
Humble yourselves before the Lord, and he will lift you up. (James 4:10)

7. We humbly asked Him to remove all our shortcomings.
If we confess our sins, he is faithful and just and will forgive us our sins and purify us from all unrighteousness. (1 John 1:9)

8. We made a list of all persons we had harmed and became willing to make amends to them all.
Do to others as you would have them do to you. (Luke 6:31)

9. We made direct amends to such people whenever possible, except when to do so would injure them or others.
Therefore, if you are offering your gift at the altar and there remember that your brother has something against you, leave your gift there in front of the altar. First go and be reconciled to your brother; then come and offer your gift. (Matt. 5:23–24)

10. We continue to take personal inventory and when we were wrong, promptly admitted it.

So, if you think you are standing firm, be careful that you don't fall! (1 Cor. 10:12)

11. We sought through prayer and meditation to improve our conscious contact with God, praying only for knowledge of His will for us, and power to carry that out.
Let the word of Christ dwell in you richly. (Col. 3:16)

12. Having had a spiritual experience as the result of these steps, we try to carry this message to others and practice these principles in all our affairs.
Brothers, if someone is caught in a sin, you who are spiritual should restore him gently. But watch yourself, or you also may be tempted. (Gal. 6:1)

Appendix 5

Recommended Resources for Your Church/Home Library

FOR ADULT MEN

Every Man's Battle:
Winning the War on Sexual Temptation One Victory at a Time
by Stephen Arterburn and Fred Stoeker

Surfing for God:
Discovering the Divine Desire Beneath Sexual Struggle
by Michael John Cusick

The Sexual Man:
Masculinity Without Guilt
by Dr. Archibald Hart

FOR ADULT WOMEN

Every Woman's Battle:
Discovering God's Plan for Sexual and Emotional Fulfillment
by Shannon Ethridge

The Sexually Confident Wife:
Connecting with Your Husband Mind, Body, Heart, Spirit
by Shannon Ethridge

FOR COUPLES

Every Man's Marriage:
An Every Man's Guide to Winning the Heart of a Woman
by Stephen Arterburn and Fred Stoeker

Every Woman's Marriage:
Igniting the Joy and Passion You Both Desire
by Shannon Ethridge

How We Love:
A Revolutionary Approach to Deeper Connections in Marriage
by Milan and Kay Yerkovich

FOR TEENS/YOUNG ADULTS

Every Young Man's Battle:
Strategies for Victory in the Real World of Sexual Temptation
by Stephen Arterburn and Fred Stoeker

Every Young Woman's Battle:
Guarding Your Mind, Heart & Body in a Sex-Saturated World
by Shannon Ethridge

FOR PARENTS

Preparing Your Son for Every Man's Battle:
Honest Conversations About Sexual Integrity
by Stephen Arterburn and Fred Stoeker

Preparing Your Daughter for Every Woman's Battle:
Creative Conversations About Sexual and Emotional Integrity
by Shannon Ethridge

How to Talk Confidently with Your Child About Sex:
For Parents (Learning About Sex)
by Lenore Buth

Notes

Introduction: Reading Between the Lions

1. Robert Johnson, *Inner Work: Using Dreams and Active Imagination for Personal Growth* (New York: Harper & Row, 1989), 95.

Chapter 1: Why Discuss Sexual Fantasies?

1. "Fantasy," Dictionary.com, http://dictionary.reference.com/browse/fantasy?s=t.
2. Neil T. Anderson, *The Bondage Breaker: Overcoming Negative Thoughts, Irrational Feelings, Habitual Sins* (Eugene, OR: Harvest House Publishers, 1993), 137.
3. Be aware that these case studies are composite sketches of many clients combined so that individual identities are protected. Any similarities between these stories and anyone you know are purely coincidental.
4. Pia Mellody is credited with introducing Jarratt Major to this concept.
5. Tina Miracle, Andrew Miracle, and Roy Baumeister, *Human Sexuality: Meeting Your Basic Needs* (Upper Saddle River, NJ: Pearson Education, Inc., 2003), 349.
6. Robin Norwood, *Daily Meditations for Women Who Love Too Much* (New York: Tarcher/Putnam, 1997), March 12.

Chapter 2: The Benefits of Boundaries

1. Tina Miracle, Andrew Miracle, and Roy Baumeister, *Human Sexuality: Meeting Your Basic Needs* (Upper Saddle River, NJ: Pearson Education, Inc., 2003), 349.
2. Ibid., 351.
3. Ibid., 352.
4. Ibid., 349.
5. "Repression," Dictionary.com, http://dictionary.reference.com/browse/repression?s=t&ld=1031.
6. "Sublimation," Dictionary.com, http://dictionary.reference.com/browse/sublimation?s=ts.
7. Gary Thomas, *Sacred Marriage* (Grand Rapids, MI: Zondervan, 2000), 222.
8. "Autoerotic," Dictionary.com, http://dictionary.reference.com/browse/autoerotic?s=t.
9. "Erotic," Dictionary.com, http://dictionary.reference.com/browse/erotic?s=t.
10. "Illicit," Dictionary.com, http://dictionary.reference.com/browse/illicit?s=t.
11. Found at http://science.howstuffworks.com/environmental/life/human-biology/brain-during-orgasm2.htm.
12. Statistics are from Brett Kahr's *Who's Been Sleeping in Your Head? The Secret World of Sexual Fantasies* (New York: Basic Books, 2008), quoted in "The Truth About Sexual Fantasies," ShoppingLifestyle.com, http://www.shoppinglifestyle.com/love/the-truth-about-sexual-fantasies/911/1.
13. Thanks to Wendy Maltz and Suzie Boss for inspiring this idea in their book *Private Thoughts: Exploring the Power of Women's Sexual Fantasies* (Charleston, SC: Booksurge, 2008), 193–95.
14. Ibid.

Chapter 3: The Faces Behind Sexual Fantasies

1. "Archetype," Dictionary.com, http://dictionary.reference.com/browse/archetypes?s=t&ld=1031.
2. Robert Johnson, *Inner Work: Using Dreams and Active Imagination for Personal Growth* (San Francisco: Harper & Row, 1986), 46.

3. Robert Bly, *A Little Book on the Human Shadow* (San Francisco: Harper & Row, 1988), 2.
4. Johnson, *Inner Work*, 50.

Chapter 4: Pornography: The Fantasy Factory

1. Elle Emmerson, "Hope for Women Living in a Porn Torn World: A Beautiful Mind," May 15, 2012, blog post, *Shannon Ethridge's Blog*; adapted from http://shannonethridge.wordpress.com/?s=A+Beautiful+Mind.
2. Chris Hedges, *Empire of Illusion: The End of Literacy and the Triumph of Spectacle* (New York: Nation Books, 2009), 68.
3. Ibid., 82.
4. Ibid., 66.
5. Ibid., 77.
6. Ibid., 59.
7. Ibid., 57.
8. ChristiaNet, Inc., "ChristiaNet Poll Finds that Evangelicals Are Addicted to Porn," MarketWire.com, August 7, 2006, http://www.marketwire.com/press-release/ChristiaNet-Poll-Finds-That-Evangelicals-Are-Addicted-to-Porn-703951.htm.
9. Dr. Michael J. Bader, *Arousal: The Secret Logic of Sexual Fantasies* (New York: Thomas Dunne Books, 2002), 5.
10. Ibid., 49.
11. Hedges, *Empire of Illusion*, 57.
12. Dr. Archibald D. Hart, *Thrilled to Death: How the Endless Pursuit of Pleasure Is Leaving Us Numb* (Nashville, TN: Thomas Nelson Publishers, 2007), 129–30, emphasis in original.
13. Ibid., 132.

Chapter 5: Bartering with Our Bodies

1. Leanne Payne, *The Broken Image* (Grand Rapids, MI: Baker Books, 1995), 42.
2. Personal e-mail to the author.
3. Timothy Keller, *Counterfeit Gods: The Empty Promises of Money, Sex, and Power, and the Only Hope That Matters* (New York: Riverhead Books, 2009), xxvi.

4. C. S. Lewis, *A Complete Guide to His Life and Works*, ed. Walter Hooper (New York: HarperCollins, 1996), 321.
5. "El Shaddai—The Breasted One," Good News Inc., http://www.goodnewsinc.net/v4gn/shaddai.html.

Chapter 6: When "One Flesh" Isn't Enough Flesh

1. Statistics are from Brett Kahr's *Who's Been Sleeping in Your Head? The Secret World of Sexual Fantasies* (New York: Basic Books, 2008), quoted in "The Truth About Sexual Fantasies," ShoppingLifestyle.com, http://www.shoppinglifestyle.com/love/the-truth-about-sexual-fantasies/911/1.
2. Ibid.
3. "What Are Dreams?" *NOVA*, produced and directed by Charles Coville, aired June 29, 2011, on PBS.
4. Dr. Harry W. Schaumburg, *False Intimacy: Understanding the Struggle of Sexual Addiction* (Colorado Springs: NavPress, 1992), 79–80.
5. Benjamin Franklin, *Autobiography and Writings* (New York: Oxford University Press, 1999), 282.
6. Shanna Freeman, "What Happens in the Brain During an Orgasm?" How Stuff Works, http://science.howstuffworks.com/environmental/life/human-biology/brain-during-orgasm2.htm.
7. Ibid.
8. Ibid.
9. Gary Thomas, *Sacred Marriage* (Grand Rapids, MI: Zondervan, 2000), 218.
10. Ibid., 226, emphasis in original.

Chapter 7: Grappling with Gay and Lesbian Fantasies

1. Louann Brizendine, *The Female Brain* (London: Bantam Books, 2006), 237–38.
2. Alex Witchel, "Life After 'Sex,'" *New York Times*, January 19, 2012, http://www.nytimes.com/2012/01/22/magazine/cynthia-nixon-wit.html?_r=1.
3. M. Pollak, "Male Homosexuality," in *Western Sexuality: Practice and Precept in Past and Present Times*, ed. Philippe Aries and Andre Bejin, trans. Anthony Forster (New York: B. Blackwell, 1985),

40–61, cited by Joseph Nicolosi in *Reparative Therapy of Male Homosexuality* (Northvale. NJ: Jason Aronson, 1991), 124, 125, found at http://www.frc.org/get.cfm?i=IS04C02#edn7.

4. David H. Demo et al., eds., *Handbook of Family Diversity* (New York: Oxford University Press, 2000), 73. Found at http://www.frc.org/get.cfm?i=IS04C02#edn7.
5. "Gay Rights: Facts About Homosexuality," FaithFacts.org, http://www.faithfacts.org/christ-and-the-culture/gay-rights#ravages.
6. "Extent, Nature, and Consequences of Intimate Partner Violence," *U.S. Department of Justice: Office of Justice Programs*, 30; "Intimate Partner Violence," *Bureau of Justice Statistics Special Report*, 11, found at http://www.frc.org/get.cfm?i=IS04C02#edn7.
7. A. P. Bell and M. S. Weinberg, *Homosexualities: A Study of Diversity Among Men and Women* (New York: Simon and Schuster, 1978), 308, 309; see also A. P. Bell, M. S. Weinberg, and S. K. Hammersmith, *Sexual Preference* (Bloomington: Indiana University Press, 1981), found at http://www.frc.org/get.cfm?i=IS04C02#edn7.
8. "Lesbian Bed Death," Wikipedia.com, http://en.wikipedia.org/wiki/Lesbian_bed_death.
9. Kevin Caruso, "Lesbian, Gay, Bisexual and Transgender Suicide," Suicide.org, http://www.suicide.org/gay-and-lesbian-suicide.html.
10. "Gay Rights," FaithFacts.org.

Chapter 8: Our Fascination with Pleasure, Pain, and Power

1. Carol Thurston, *The Romance Revolution* (Chicago: University of Illinois Press, 1987), 78; Michael Castleman, "Women's Rape Fantasies: How Common? What Do They Mean?" PsychologyToday.com, http://www.psychologytoday.com/blog/all-about-sex/201001/womens-rape-fantasies-how-common-what-do-they-mean.
2. Dr. Michael J. Bader, *Arousal: The Secret Logic of Sexual Fantasies* (New York: Thomas Dunne Books, 2002), 126–27.
3. Ibid., 127.

4. Robert Johnson, *Inner Work: Using Dreams and Active Imagination for Personal Growth* (San Francisco: Harper & Row, 1986), 71.
5. Bader, *Arousal*, 130.
6. Etty Hillesum, *Etty: The Letters and Diaries of Etty Hillesum, 1941–1943* (Grand Rapids: Eerdmans, 2002), 529.
7. Statistics are from Brett Kahr's *Who's Been Sleeping in Your Head? The Secret World of Sexual Fantasies* (New York: Basic Books, 2008), quoted in "The Truth About Sexual Fantasies," ShoppingLifestyle.com, http://www.shoppinglifestyle.com/love/the-truth-about-sexual-fantasies/911/1.
8. Shanna Freeman, "What Happens in the Brain During an Orgasm?" How Stuff Works, http://science.howstuffworks.com/environmental/life/human-biology/brain-during-orgasm2.htm.
9. Bader, *Arousal*, 113.
10. Personal e-mail to the author.
11. Chris Hedges, *Empire of Illusion: The End of Literacy and the Triumph of Spectacle* (New York: Nation Books, 2009), 74, 86, 87.
12. Robert Bly, *A Little Book on the Human Shadow* (San Francisco: Harper & Row, 1988), 9–10.

Chapter 9: Putting Fantasy in Its Place

1. Leanne Payne, *The Broken Image* (Grand Rapids, MI: Baker Books, 1995), 30.
2. Ann Voskamp, *One Thousand Gifts* (Grand Rapids, MI: Zondervan, 2010), 216–17.

Conclusion: The Rest of the Story

1. I wrote about the concept of embracing your role as the bride of Christ in my book, *Completely His: Loving Jesus Without Limits* (Colorado Springs, CO: WaterBrook Press, 2007).

Appendix 2: Curing the Sexual Abuse Epidemic

1. Lynda S. Doll, Linda J. Koenig, and David W. Purcell, "Child Sexual Abuse and Adult Sexual Risk: Where Are We Now?" in *From Child Sexual Abuse to Adult Sexual Risk*, ed. Lynda S. Doll et al. (Washington, DC: American Psychological Association, 2004), 3–10; Shanta R. Dube et al., "Long-Term Consequences

of Childhood Sexual Abuse by Gender of Victim," *American Journal of Preventive Medicine* 28, no. 5 (2005): 430–38; David M. Fergusson, L. John Horwood, and Michael T. Lynskey, "Childhood Sexual Abuse, Adolescent Sexual Behavior, and Sexual Revictimization," *Child Abuse & Neglect* 21 (August 1997): 789–803; David Finkelhor and Jennifer Dziuba-Leatherman, "Children as Victims of Violence: A National Survey," *Pediatrics* 94 (October 1994): 413–20; Jim Hooper, *Child Abuse: Statistics, Research, Resources* (Boston: Boston University School of Medicine, 1998); Cynthia Simpson, Rebecca K. Odor, and Saba Masho, *Childhood Sexual Assault Victimization in Virginia* (Richmond, VA: Center for Injury and Violence Prevention, Virginia Department of Health, 2004).

2. Gene G. Abel and Nora Harlow, *Stop Child Molestation Book* (published by the authors, 2001); Dean G. Kilpatrick, Benjamin E. Saunders, and Daniel W. Smith, *Youth Victimization: Prevalence and Implications*, (Washington, DC: U.S. Department of Justice, Office of Justice Programs, National Institute of Justice, 2003); Howard N. Snyder, *Sexual Assault of Young Children as Reported to Law Enforcement: Victim, Incident, and Offender Characteristics* (Washington, DC: U.S. Department of Justice, Bureau of Justice Statistics, 2000).
3. Michele Elliott, Kevin Browne, and Jennifer Kilcoyne, "Child Sexual Abuse Prevention: What Offenders Tell Us," *Child Abuse & Neglect* 5 (May 1995), 579–94; Abel and Harlow, *Stop Child Molestation Book*; Kilpatrick, Saunders, and Smith, *Youth Victimization*.
4. Andrea J. Sedlak et al., *Fourth National Incidence Study of Child Abuse and Neglect (NIS-4)*, Report to Congress (Washington, DC: U.S. Department of Health and Human Services, Administration for Children and Families, 2010), 3–9.
5. Gene G. Abel et al., "Self-Reported Sex Crimes on Nonincarcerated Paraphiliacs," *Journal of Interpersonal Violence* 2 (March 1987): 3–25; Kilpatrick, Saunders, and Smith, *Youth Victimization*.
6. Abel et al., ibid.

Appendix 4: Twelve Steps to Recovery

1. John Baker, adapted from *The Big Book of Alcoholics Anonymous* (Grand Rapids, MI: Zondervan, 1998).

About the Author

Shannon Ethridge is a best-selling author, international speaker, and certified life coach with a master's degree in counseling/human relations from Liberty University. She is the author of nineteen books, including the million-copy best-selling Every Woman's Battle series, the five-book Completely His series, and *The Sexually Confident Wife*.

Shannon is a frequent guest on television and radio programs, such as *The Today Show*, *The 700 Club*, *New Life Live!* with Stephen Arterburn, and *Life Today* with James and Betty Robison. She also mentors aspiring writers and speakers through her B.L.A.S.T. program (Building Leaders, Authors, Speakers, and Teachers). Shannon lives in Tyler, Texas, with her husband, Greg, and their children, Erin and Matthew.

Learn more at **www.ShannonEthridge.com**.

If you enjoyed *The Fantasy Fallacy*,
look for Shannon's fiction debut
coauthored with Kathy Mackel

To Know You

Julia must face the wounds
of her past to secure
her family's future.

AVAILABLE OCTOBER 2013